An Issue of Blood
Facing Uterine Cancer With Faith

An Issue of Blood
Facing Uterine Cancer With Faith

Jean C. Fischer

Unless otherwise noted, bible verses are from THE HOLY BIBLE, NEW INTERNATIONAL VERSION®, NIV® Copyright © 1973, 1978, 1984, 2011 by Biblica, Inc.® Used by permission. All rights reserved worldwide.

The information in this book is for educational purposes only and not intended as a substitute for professional medical advice. Readers should consult their health-care physicians regarding their own individual medical conditions and treatment plans.

The names of doctors and others have been obscured or changed to protect their privacy.

Copyright © 2013 Jean C. Fischer

All rights reserved. No part of this book may be reproduced in any form whatsoever without written permission from the author except by reviewers quoting brief passages in articles, blogs, or reviews

ISBN-10:1492321354
ISBN-13:978-1492321354

DEDICATION

For Mom.
You encouraged me, inspired me, and supported me.
I miss you.

CONTENTS

FOREWORD Important Information 1

PART ONE Gathering Risks 5

PART TWO Living Through Cancer 41

PART THREE Facing the Future 131

PART FOUR Life After Cancer 171

ACKNOWLEDGMENTS

Thank you to my doctors and their staffs, the nurses at the hospital, and especially to Sarah and Chuck, my family, friends, everyone who prayed me through the valleys, and most of all to my Heavenly Father who healed me and led me to write this book.

Foreword
Important Information

How much do you know about uterine cancer? Can you list its symptoms? Do you know what puts you at risk? Do you know that endometrial (uterine) cancer is the fourth most common cancer among women in the United States or that it most often occurs in older women? I certainly didn't. Until I was diagnosed in 2010, I knew nothing about it. I thought that the symptoms I experienced in my late fifties were normal signs of menopause. But they weren't.

Before I share my story with you, there are a few things that I want you to know, facts that might save your life or the life of someone you love. These facts are so important that I've put them at the beginning of my book so that you can easily find them. I know that too many facts and figures can be boring so I'll keep it brief, but please don't skip over this part.

About 95% of cancers of the uterus are endometrial cancers—cancers affecting the uterine lining. It was estimated that in 2013, the year this book was written, there would be roughly 49,500 new cases of uterine cancer. Of those, only 8,000 would be fatal. Diagnostic tools and treatments have constantly improved and so has the mortality rate. Often, endometrial cancer has a high rate of cure, between 83 – 96% if caught early.

Symptoms include:

- Vaginal bleeding after menopause
- Bleeding between periods
- An abnormal, watery or blood-tinged discharge from the vagina
- Pelvic pain
- Pain during intercourse

Conditions other than cancer can cause these symptoms, but to be on the safe side, call your doctor if you experience any of them, especially if you are older than fifty. If you believe that an annual PAP test will detect uterine cancer, think again. Very few cases are found through PAPs. This is why it is so important to report to your doctor if you experience any unusual symptoms.

According to the CDC, there is no way to know for sure if you will get uterine cancer. However, these factors may increase your risk:

- Being older than 50.
- Being obese (having a high amount of extra body fat).
- Taking estrogen alone for hormone replacement during menopause (without also taking progesterone).
- Having had trouble getting pregnant or fewer than five periods in a year at any time before starting menopause.
- Taking Tamoxifen, a drug used to treat certain types of breast cancer.
- Having people in your family with a history of uterine, colon, or ovarian cancer.

You can have some of these risks and never get uterine cancer, or you can get uterine cancer even if you don't have any of the risks. Awareness is the key to catching it in its earliest stages when it can be cured. Some forms of uterine cancer progress quickly and can be deadly, so please don't wait. It is best to check with your doctor if you think that something might be wrong.

For most of my life, I unknowingly lived with some of the risk factors. In fact, my journey with uterine cancer began more than forty years ago on the day of my first period, the day I started collecting risks that could alter my life forever. In my story, I will tell you about why I think I was at risk, how my Christian faith brought me through the diagnosis and treatment, and what my life is like after cancer. Hopefully, you will find my story an easy read and even a bit humorous at times. Above all, I hope that it will increase your awareness of uterine cancer and encourage you. My prayer is that you will live your life without ever experiencing uterine cancer. But if you do get it, don't despair. Many women with uterine cancer live a normal lifespan and die of causes other than their cancer. Today, there are more than 500,000 uterine cancer survivors, and I am grateful to be one of them.

> I will not die but live, and will proclaim
> what the LORD has done.
> —Psalm 118:17

Part One – Gathering Risks

CHAPTER 1
Mother Daughter Talk

Cancer. That word crosses the threshold of our conversations way too often. The idea of cancer envelops us. Its ravaging effects become the theme of news stories, movies, documentaries, and television dramas. The hope for a cure appears in ads soliciting and offering support. Celebrities sing the birthday song to wish cancer survivors many more years living cancer free, and still, some of us find ourselves in cancer's bull's-eye. "Jean, you have cancer." I've felt the sting of those four simple words.

The media attention has not been a bad thing because it increases people's awareness. Today, men, women, children, no one can escape the word *cancer*, but, if nothing else, we are better informed than any previous generation about its risks and prevention. But this wasn't true in the 1960s when I entered my teens. Back then, doctors didn't know that an early menses might signal a higher risk of uterine cancer later in life. In fact, in the 1960s there was little information about cancer's risks.

Early menstruation was something silently celebrated, a rite of passage shared between mothers and daughters. My story begins on that day when my mother and I shared the secret.

Every girl anticipates the life changing moment when she gets her period. Mine came on a hot summer day while I played on the beach with my friends. A sudden twinge and a strange feeling "down there" sent me rushing home. Girls my age didn't discuss periods. I wonder even now if the friends I played with that day knew as much about menstruation as I did.

In my elementary school, I had attended a special half-hour health class for third-grade girls. A parent's permission was required, and I had permission, but some of my girlfriends didn't. Their parents found the class inappropriate. Our teacher, Mrs. Reed, taught us the basics of puberty and introduced us, in the most innocuous way, to the concept of menstruation (in other words "your time of the month" or "feeling a little under the weather"). We learned that during a menstrual period a woman bleeds from her womb. We discovered that a period lasts from three to seven days, and each period commences approximately every twenty-eight days.

"Menstruation is an important part of growing up," Mrs. Reed said. "All ladies menstruate, and it's nothing to be afraid of. Some girls know about menstruation, and others don't. So, please keep it quiet. Don't ever discuss menstruation in public; it's not lady-like. And never, ever talk about menstruation with boys."

She gave us a brochure that showed a sanitary napkin and a tampon, and she explained only that these products kept the blood from staining a woman's underpants. She referred to these things as being "like a bandage." Then she gave each girl a large sealed envelope to take home to her mother. It held a little booklet that we could share together when the time was right.

When I arrived home from the beach that day, I locked myself in the bathroom, and I discovered a small amount of bright red blood on my underpants. Knowing that it was my period, in a rush of frightened euphoria I called to my mother, "Mom, I'm bleeding! But just a little."

My mother stood at the kitchen stove frying liver and onions. I guess when she heard my cry she thought that I'd cut myself playing outside or that I had fallen off my bike and skinned a knee, both common when you're eleven.

"Wash it good and spray it with Bactine."

Huh? Wash it and spray it with a disinfectant? I didn't think so. I unlocked the bathroom door and walked to the kitchen. "Mom, I'm bleeding! You know . . . down there." I pointed toward my waist.

My mother shifted her attention from the frying pan to me. "Oh," she said, wide-eyed. And then after a few seconds, *"Oh!"*

I think every mother has a fleeting moment of disbelief and then maybe sadness when her daughter says the words: "I'm bleeding down there." It signals the beginning of the end of childhood. That one spot of blood ushers in a new era of raging hormones, boys, and dating. I can't know what thoughts tumbled through Mom's head that day, but she got a pair of clean underpants from my dresser drawer and went with me into the bathroom where she taught me how to put on a thin elastic belt and a Modess pad. Modess was a leading brand of sanitary napkin in the sixties.

The choices of feminine hygiene products were few. Adhesive pads that stuck to the crotch of your underwear hadn't been invented yet. I think those came along in the seventies. Preteen girls, like myself, rarely used tampons. Even thinking about how and where to insert them made most girls shudder. The weapon of choice against bloodstains was a garter belt with one metal fastener in the front and another in back. The sanitary napkins had long, narrow tails on each end that slipped securely into the fasteners. Some belts even came with a shield, a moisture-resistant panel that prevented accidents. Imagine something that looked like Tarzan's loincloth, but stark white and a bit shorter. The garter belt hugged a woman's middle. Sometimes it caused a rashy irritation where it rubbed against her skin. Still, garter belts were a far cry from the rags and safety pins of my grandmother's era, or the rabbit, caribou and other animal skins once used by our ancient female ancestors.

Picture this: In centuries past, women sometimes relied on natural products like grass and moss to collect their blood, or horrors—nothing at all. I've read that before the 19th century many women just went with the flow; they bled into their clothing! Aren't you grateful that you live in the 21st century?

After my Modess pad was securely in place, Mom took me

into her bedroom and showed me another nifty item that she had tucked away in the back of her underwear drawer. She said that if I wanted one, she would get it for me. "It" turned out to be a pair of innocent looking rayon panties, but on closer inspection I saw that the crotch was made of a thin plastic fabric. Sewn into it were two fasteners placed a perfect distance apart to hold the sanitary napkin's tails.

"I'll get you some plastic panties to wear at bedtime," Mom promised in a hushed voice. "They protect against embarrassing accidents."

A diaper! No way. I knew that I'd get my period someday, but nobody told me that it came with all this special equipment. I tried to decide which was more disgusting, the belt and pad or the plastic undies.

"Now what?" I asked my mother. "Do I have to stay inside?"

A girlfriend had whispered to me that her older and wiser sister told her that girls with periods shouldn't take baths or showers. Since they couldn't bathe they had to stay indoors until their time of the month ended— *because they stunk!* And I believed her. Now that I had my period, I figured that it was time to start asking my mom some questions.

Something had happened to me at a Christmas Day dinner when I was nine, something that had trumped the third-grade health class. While it had embarrassed me, it also made me aware that Mom was open to questions about "that time of the month," at least about the basics.

On that Christmas Day, my grandmothers, my great-aunt and uncle, my parents and I sat around our dining room table. If you haven't guessed, I'm an only child. As we devoured a twenty-pound turkey, Great Uncle Walter asked for another dinner napkin, and Mom sent me to the kitchen to get it. There weren't any.

"Mom?" I called out, but my mother didn't answer.

The grownups were engaged in a heated debate about the Kennedy administration.

"Mom?" Nothing.

Then I remembered that I had seen a bulky package stuffed behind a stack of bath towels in the bathroom linen closet. It had the word *napkins* printed on its sides. When I checked it out I noticed another word, this one unfamiliar. I spelled it. S-A-N-I-T-A-R-Y. I tried sounding it out putting the emphasis on each syllable. Sań-i-tar-y. *Sanitary!* I knew that word. I'd heard it at school in Health class. It meant clean. "Boys and girls, it is very important to be sanitary. After using the bathroom remember to wash your hands with lots of soap and water." Sanitary napkins, I decided, must mean clean napkins! Inside the package were a bunch of soft, thick paper things. They weren't like any napkin that I had ever seen. But, hey! Uncle Walter needed a napkin, and these should work. In my little girl brain I decided that sanitary napkins were special napkins used for cleaning your hands after you went to the bathroom. Why hadn't anyone told me about this? I grabbed a napkin out of the package, trotted back to the table, and I presented it to my Uncle Walter.

Now, you have to understand that my great-uncle was in his sixties, ancient as far as I was concerned. And, although he was a bit eccentric, he was also an introvert. When he saw what I'd brought him, his neck turned fiery red. The scarlet glow crept up his cheeks and washed over his forehead. Finally, it slipped under the last remaining white hairs on his almost bald head. The poor man was befuddled and embarrassed.

Aunt Clara stifled a giggle, and Grandma Lily, my dad's mother, broke out in raucous laughter. Soon, everyone at the table hooted and hollered and held their sides.

"What's so funny?" I said, tears burning in my eyes. "Why are you laughing at me?"

Grandma Dorothy saw the tears and tried to rescue me.

"It's my fault, Sweetie."

She managed to get the words out, trying hard not to laugh.

"I felt like a hee-hee's egg in a ha-ha's nest, and that just got me to laughing."

Grandma Dorothy liked that expression, a hee-hee's egg in a ha-ha's nest. She used it a lot.

"And that got all of us to laughing," Grandma Lily added, trying desperately to help.

Uncle Walter, whose color had almost returned to normal, said nothing. Nor did my dad. Walter slipped the sanitary napkin under the table to my mother, and the conversation turned to whether we all had room for Grandma's Dutch apple pie.

That night, after we'd put the dinner dishes away, Mom and I had the talk, or at least part of it. She explained what sanitary napkins were for, and she told me not to tell my friends. I felt confused afterward and mortified that I had made such a dumb mistake as to give one of those things to my poor, old uncle.

I think the Great Christmas Day Incident of 1961 had a lot to do with my mom allowing me to attend that third-grade health class, but still, two years later at age eleven I had only a few pieces of the menstruation puzzle. I knew that women had certain days of each month when they bled down there. I knew that they wore a bandage called a sanitary napkin or some weird cardboard thing called a tampon.

Mom told me more about menstruation in those years between nine and eleven, but not a lot. I learned that bleeding had something to do with being able to have a baby when I got married. Then when I was a little older, mom warned me that I would probably start bleeding sooner than later. She said that most girls started in their early teens.

But I still didn't know why women bled. Did I really want to know what terrible thing happened once a month to make a woman bleed? I held that question for another time when I would be closer to becoming a woman. In the meantime I suffered silently, terrified of that day when my period would start and yet eager for it to happen.

Answering my question about staying indoors, Mom said, "You can do everything you usually do except swim."

"For how long?" I asked.

"Until your period stops."

It made sense. If you couldn't take a bath or shower when you had your period, then you probably shouldn't swim either. Water was water, after all. What a puzzle was this thing called menstruation. A confused look must have swept over my face.

"You'll have your period all the time for a few days," Mom explained. "And while you have it, you can't wear a bathing suit or go swimming."

Sad news on a hot, July day. We lived across the street from

Lake Michigan, and in our neighborhood running around in a bathing suit and going swimming were as normal as eating and breathing. Why couldn't I get wet down there? Was it okay to take a bath? What awful thing might happen if the water accidentally touched me? These questions rushed through my mind, but I felt too embarrassed to ask them.

"So, what am I supposed to tell my friends?" I said asked. "They'll know that something's wrong if I can't go swimming."

Mom turned her attention back to the liver and onions. "Just tell them that your mother said so."

End of conversation.

Some of my girlfriends had to be menstruating already. I couldn't be the only one. I wondered which ones knew the secret. I tried to remember if any of them had made up an excuse about why she couldn't go into the water or if any had mysteriously disappeared for seven to ten days. No. None of them had. Maybe I really was the first one in my group to become a woman. An exciting, yet scary, thought.

At supper that night, my father noticed me quietly picking at my food.

"Anything going on?" he wondered.

I looked at my mother who shrugged her shoulders, smiled, and left it up to me to tell him. I considered it, but then I decided that telling my father that I'd started menstruating wasn't the best dinner table conversation.

"Are you okay?" Dad asked. "You're too quiet. Maybe you're coming down with something."

"She'll be fine," Mom said. She winked, but he missed it.

My dad, always the worrier, wasn't going to let it slide.

"She looks a little pale."

He reached over and brushed the back of his hand against my face.

I pulled away.

"And she feels warm. Do you think, maybe, we should call Doctor Pearson—"

"I'm fine!" I shouted. "I have cramps! Okay?"

I dissolved into tears and ran to my bedroom. As I lie on my bed, I heard my parents laughing. Mom had told him. He knew that I had my period, and that made me cry even harder. For the first time in my life I felt happy to be an only child. At least I didn't have to face siblings with the news of my horribly altered state. I could imagine how girls felt if they had brothers. How humiliating! Family secrets are just that—family secrets. Usually everyone in the family knows, and sometimes brothers and sisters tell. But since grownups kept menstruation such a guarded secret mine was safe with my parents. I stayed in my room embarrassed to face my father.

Just before bedtime, Mom handed me the thin, square booklet that had been sealed in its envelope since third grade. The title on the cover said: NOW YOU ARE 10, and an illustration showed a girl with auburn hair done up neatly in a ponytail and tied with a pale pink ribbon.

"Ten?" I protested.

"Some girls start that young," Mom said. "Read it. It will answer all your questions."

Then she left me alone.

I opened the cover. The first page said that soon I would take a big step in the adventure of growing up. It might happen when I was ten, or eleven, or even a few years later. The next several pages showed how a girl's body changed. Dumb stuff like as girls grew they were measured in feet instead of inches. I hoped so! And instead of a flat chest and straight hips, our bodies were developing soft, girlish curves. (This was only slightly true in my case.) Finally, on page eight, I saw the word menstruation. The booklet explained that each month a small amount of blood leaked out through the vagina, an opening in the lower part of your body. I had never heard the word *vagina*. Did I have one? Where was it? There wasn't a picture. The next sentence said I'd know when I was menstruating because I would see a small, red stain on my underclothes or bed sheet. When that happened I should tell my mother, and she would be glad to help me. She was—sort of. The rest of the pages were nothing but an ad for a brand of sanitary napkins. *Up and over, down and around.* The book said to memorize that phrase just like I had memorized bible verses in Sunday School. Once I had it in my head, I would never forget to gather the napkin ends up and over the clasp lock on the belt, then down into the clasp lock, and finally around in back. If I did this correctly I would have a nice, smooth line under my skirt or dress instead of a bulky twisted bulge that screamed to the world, "I'm menstruating!"

Congratulations on becoming a woman. This marked the end of my at-home sex education. Mom and I never again discussed the mechanics of menstruation. She'd given me the equipment, and I'd read the book. Done.

A few years later, by the time I left middle school, I knew the names of my female parts, where they were, and why I had them but only because I'd hidden among the stacks of health books at the public library and looked at pictures meant for grownups. Eventually, I learned when to expect my period, and I knew how my body would react. Menstruation became a regular part of my teenage life. Like the booklet said, I had become a woman. But I had discovered how to get there mostly on my own.

As the seventies approached, teen girls talked more openly about their periods. By the time I entered high school, I'd learned that humans had seeds and eggs, and someday a man's seed might fertilize one of my eggs. If that happened a baby would grow inside my uterus. I also knew that someday when I grew old (to me old was in your fifties) my uterus would stop working as an incubator. It would rest inside me dormant and no longer produce its monthly share of blood. Still, I figured that it would remain a part of me all the days of my life. I never thought that, one day, I would lose it to cancer.

I couldn't know back then that by starting my period before the age of twelve I was at a higher risk for getting uterine cancer. I couldn't know that I would gather more risk factors as I went through life. Nor could I know that by the time cancer invaded my body I would be a committed Christian and cancer would toughen my faith to where I would finally surrender all to God.

Until that day when cancer struck, my ignorance was bliss.

CHAPTER 2
Colliding With Cancer Head-On

"Jean, you have cancer." The diagnosis came three months after my fifty-eighth birthday. When my doctor said those words, numbness fell on me hard. I stood outside myself emotionless, robotic, observing the scene unfolding in my gynecologist's office. What a strange reaction for a woman who worried every detail. When thrust into a crisis my brain typically whirled with what-ifs, if-onlies, and untold questions starved for answers. But when I heard the word cancer along with my name, I felt nothing. In a heartbeat, I escaped to a place deep within me, a cold, dark, familiar cavern, a virtual tomb.

Do you like old cemeteries? Maybe that's a silly question. Does anyone like cemeteries? I enjoy traipsing around in them ferreting out ancient headstones.

Tucked away on a hill in Green Ridge Cemetery you'll find my favorite old headstone, a mid-nineteenth century monument. The name of the deceased has long since weathered away. A chiseled angel embraces the stone, head bowed, one frail cheek resting on the stone's crown. If you study her face, you'll see that she weeps, a single tear frozen in time. The years have almost worn it away, but it's there, a testament that grief never completely ends but softens the further it travels from death.

By the time I was diagnosed I had already suffered the grief that cancer brings. Cancer had come near to me. Now when it stalked me, I retreated to the hidden place where memories lie buried.

My conscious relationship with cancer began in the 1970s when I was in my twenties. That's when I met a woman my age named Rose. We became fast friends, in retrospect too fast. Rose's father had died of brain cancer when Rose was just nineteen. Her mother died of lung cancer seven years later. Neither parent had lived long enough to hold their first grandchild, a baby girl named Meagan. Rose gave birth to Meagan two months after her mother died. Can you imagine going to your mother's funeral when you're seven months pregnant with your first child, your mother's only grandchild, hiccupping and kicking inside of you? Adding to her pain, Rose had a much younger sister who still needed parenting. After their parents' deaths, Rose became her guardian.

That first day when Rose and I met, she asked me an odd question.

"Are your folks still living?"

Weren't everyone's parents alive? "Sure," I told her.

"You're lucky," said Rose. "I'm an orphan. Mom died two years ago, and Daddy's been gone five years."

What person in her twenties describes herself as an orphan? But that was Rose. I was too young and unscathed by life's unpleasant realities to understand that cancer is an insidious rogue that preys not only on its victims, but also their families. Cancer sometimes makes orphans, and Cancer always hangs out with Fear. Cancer breaks in, and then Fear strikes stone-cold hard.

Rose was in every sense an orphan. In typography, an orphan is a word at the end of a paragraph left dangling at the bottom of a column, a word separated from the rest. That was Rose: a young, married, twenty-six-year-old mother separated from her parents and left dangling in this thing called life. Cancer had busted through the back door, murdered her mom and dad, and made her an orphan. Fear left Rose damaged. She behaved and thought differently from many women her age whose parents were alive and well, parents who worked a little, golfed a little, and enjoyed the freedom of an empty nest. In Rose there was an inner pallor that grazed the surface of her otherwise spunky personality. She could be wildly social and almost rowdy and just as frequently withdrawn and afflicted. Her moodiness was beyond my understanding. In fact, it affected our friendship so negatively that finally we parted ways. Had Cancer done this to Rose? Had Fear numbed her until her emotions broke loose in a freefall?

Cancer was the last thing on my mind when I was Rose's age. Nobody I knew had it. I thought only old people died from it. At twenty-six, I had just begun to live, and to me life meant a career, a husband, children, and after that only good things. Isn't that the way life is supposed to be? You fall in love, get married, have kids, and then you retire to sunny Florida. You sip margaritas on a sandy beach and finally, when you are really old and really tired and only when there's no living left to do, that's when you die—and maybe from cancer.

But, the truth is that life isn't always good. God allows trials to enter our lives, valleys designed to draw us nearer to Him and to build our faith. One day we all will die, and some of us will die from cancer. It's how we approach life that matters.

Back in the seventies, I was an agnostic. Had I known Jesus then, I would have accepted the fact that difficulties are a part of God's plan.

In John 16:33, Jesus says, "In this world you will have trouble." He doesn't say, "You might have trouble." He says, "You *will* have trouble." Guaranteed. All of us will have trouble sooner or later. But the second part of John 16:33 holds a powerful promise. Jesus goes on to say: "But take heart! I have overcome the world." Did you notice that He used the past tense? "I *have* overcome the world." Isn't that an awesome thought? When bad things happen, like cancer, we know that Jesus has already conquered it. What we endure here on Earth is temporary. If we believe that Jesus died for our sins, then we know that someday we will have eternal life with Him in Heaven, a place free of anything bad, free of diseases.

Jesus had already conquered everything bad that would ever come into my life, but as a young woman in my twenties and an agnostic, Fear kept me from accepting that as truth. If you think about it, the words *agnostic* and *fear* are synonyms.

I had studied music in college and planned to be a band

director. Then I dropped out of the music program and decided to be an elementary school teacher. That idea held until the very end of my senior year when I took a required course in children's literature. I wondered why I had waited so long to rediscover *Make Way for Ducklings*, the *Poky Little Puppy* and *Paddle-to-the-Sea*. My plan shifted again. Instead of applying for teaching jobs after graduation, I went on to graduate school and earned a master's degree in Library Science and Children's Literature. From there, I had no idea where I would go. Did I want to work in a public library? Teach? Write? I navigated an ever-changing life course overflowing with dead-ends and detours. Lost in an agnostic sea without a compass I tried to find my way home. Meanwhile, my parents' lives were changing, too. They had entered a new life-phase, caring for their elderly mothers.

Grandma Lily, Dad's mom, lived in the upper flat of their duplex. When I was little, Grandma had been my baby-sitter and my rainy-day friend. We played cards and board games together. She even let me hang out with her once-a-month, church-ladies Bunco club. Her white-haired friends doted on me and thought I was "as cute as a bug's ear." I couldn't imagine being without Grandma Lily.

But in her old age, Grandma became stubborn and feisty. She criticized my long hair and washed out bell-bottomed blue jeans. She didn't like the round-framed granny glasses that I wore or that I chose the Rolling Stones over the Osmond Brothers. I began avoiding this new grandma whose mind drifted, this grandma with scraggly yellow-white hair and clothing that sometimes smelled. My folks had to remind her to bathe, change her underwear, and even to use the bathroom. That's when I bailed. I left my family and their issues behind, and I moved thirty miles away to a college dormitory.

I wasn't home the night the rescue squad came, and I wasn't at the hospital when Mom and Dad sat by Grandma's bedside. When I got the call, I was in the dorm's game room playing ping-pong with a boy I'd just met and wanted to date. My roommate yelled to me from our room down the hall.

"Jean, your dad's on the phone."

"Tell him I'll call him later," I shouted.

"He wants to talk to you *now*."

I remember tossing the ping-pong paddle onto the table and asking, almost begging, the boy to wait for me. I went to my dorm room, picked up the phone, and in the most annoyed tone I said, "So, Dad, what's going on?"

There was a brief pause. "Grandma Lily died."

This was my first headstone moment. Numbness struck me. I couldn't cry. I couldn't feel. I barely heard myself say, "I'm not coming home. I'd rather remember her as she was." I left out because I'm too afraid to face death head on.

"No," Dad insisted. "I'm coming there to get you."

Grandma wanted a private funeral with a closed casket. I felt grateful for that. I didn't want to see her dead. If I didn't have to look at death, then I could hang onto my illusion of immortality. I said to myself, I'll be active in my old age. I'll run marathons and certainly not be grumpy and forgetful, and definitely not ragged and smelly. I'll die peacefully in my sleep, but not until I'm a hundred and five. I ambled through Grandma Lily's funeral like an anesthetized spectator. Bad things happened to other people, but not to my family. Still, two years later something bad did happen to my family. We had more trouble, and this time it was cancer.

In 1976, Grandma Dorothy got very sick and ended up in the hospital. She couldn't keep food down, she lost a lot of weight, and her skin took on a jaundiced pallor. The doctor told my mother and her siblings that he suspected cancer, but they decided not to tell Grandma. The doctor said that surgery would confirm his diagnosis. So her children took a wait and see approach. No use adding to Grandma's worries. "You'll be fine," they told her. "Remember your gall bladder surgery? That turned out okay, and this will, too." They led her into the half-truth that she had a bile duct obstruction. I understand now why they lied to their mother. They were afraid to face cancer head-on. There's that word again *afraid*.

I've decided that Fear is a god that we bow down to. It grabs on and holds us hostage, and too often we give in to it. I'm guilty of it. You might be, too. I sometimes capitalize the word *fear* in this book because, if we allow it, Fear can become more than just a concept. It controls us and lives in our hearts—if we allow it. The same is true of Cancer.

In Isaiah 41:10, God says to Jacob, "Fear not, for I am with you; Be not dismayed, for I am your God. I will strengthen you, Yes, I will help you, I will uphold you with My righteous right hand." (NKJV) That's God talking to us, telling us not to be afraid. It doesn't get any better than that. Did you notice that God uses the present tense? He says, "I *am* with you." How do we know that He is with us? Because in Revelation 1:8 God says, "I am the Alpha and the Omega . . .who is, and who was, and who is to come, the Almighty." Our Almighty God is right here with us, and He can strike down Fear just as easily now as He could in Jacob's time. I know that now, but I didn't when Grandma Dorothy got sick.

I lived with my parents then, in Grandma Lily's upstairs flat. This time, I couldn't avoid thinking about death. It shrouded me. Nothing else existed. I stood facing it like Shadrach, Meshach, and Abednego at King Nebuchadnezzar's furnace. Only then, I didn't know the ending to that bible story. I didn't have a personal relationship with the God who saved those three men's lives.

When the surgeon opened Grandma's body and looked inside, he discovered the cancer was much worse than he'd thought. Her stomach, pancreas, bowels, and liver were riddled with the disease. He removed as much of it as he could, and then he told us that Grandma Dorothy would die, maybe not that day or the next, but soon. No radiation. No chemotherapy. No remission, and no cure. I had to face the truth then—cancer kills people, and it could kill the ones I loved. It might even kill me.

So what did I do? I built a wall between Cancer and myself. Like a machine performing a precise series of tasks, I did what I had to do. Still, I would not allow myself to feel the fear and the suffering that comes with cancer. Subconsciously I vowed that something that vile and evil would never get inside of me. Today, I call this my "robot mode." When I met Cancer dead-on, I escaped into the empty cavern of my soul, and I hid there until I thought it was safe to come out.

It surprised me that my mother and her siblings chose not to tell Grandma her prognosis. After surgery when she came out of the anesthesia, they continued telling her that she'd had a bile duct obstruction. They even made plans to bring her home.

Fear does that. It leads you to dodge the truth and run from facing the inevitable. Every one of us will die. That means you and me. When death comes too close to us, we instinctively want to run away with Fear, and that's what my family did. They ran, and so did I.

Grandma Dorothy never came home. She languished for several months, first in the hospital and then a nursing home. Finally, one day, she looked into my mother's eyes and mine, and she whispered, "I love you my darlings." That evening, she went to be with the Lord. I had been present during my grandmother's journey toward heaven, and I saw what Cancer does. I had witnessed a cancer death, and I had no choice but to accept that life isn't always rosy.

A few years after Grandma Dorothy died I found out that she'd known about her cancer. Her best friend, a dear lady named Libby, had told her. Libby and Grandma kept it a secret because Grandma didn't want to upset her children even more. She didn't want to add to their troubles as they stood helplessly watching Cancer rob them of their mother. I've regretted that I didn't tell Grandma Dorothy myself. I'd thought about it back then. I wish that I had told her, because I missed out on saying goodbye and a hundred other things.

I understand now why Rose's emotions had swung wild. Rose was suffering from a cancer hangover. Cancer hangovers are a common problem both for survivors of cancer and also for the families of those who died. And it takes a while to get rid of them.

Throughout Grandma Dorothy's illness, I felt trapped in an abusive relationship with a disease that beat up our family. Nothing I'd done, not even begging God (even agnostics do that), could save Grandma from Cancer's steadfast grip. I felt powerless over it. Cancer killed my Grandma Dorothy, and it left me crushed and afraid. If I allowed myself to think about it I could imagine being an orphan like Rose. Cancer could absolutely kill my parents just as it had hers. Those cancerous thoughts played over and over in my head until they found their place in my memories.

Without faith, colliding with Cancer head-on is like being thrown into a fiery furnace. Its heat not only destroys the body, but it sears the soul and leaves it scarred.

In 2010 when my doctor told me that I had uterine cancer, he explained that it usually strikes women after menopause, and in its earliest stages it's almost always curable. "However," he said, "We won't know for sure until we get in there and see what's going on." Those words *we won't know for sure* were enough to allow old memories to seep into my consciousness. I ran away then with Fear to my hidden place where I could bask in comfortable numbness.

Thank God I wasn't an agnostic when I got cancer. This time when I escaped to The Hidden Place, God's words echoed there. He spoke the familiar words of Jeremiah 29:11, "'For I know the plans I have for you . . .plans to prosper you and not to harm you, plans to give you hope and a future.'" But even as a Christian, the relationship that I'd already formed with Cancer made it difficult for me to face having it and to believe in a positive outcome. When I found myself at a vulnerable age in my late fifties attacked by uterine cancer, the ugly, stagnant memories of Grandma Dorothy's cancer made me afraid.

Back in the 1970s when Grandma had cancer, the word *cancer* often meant a death sentence. Much of the technology and many of the treatments that we have today were experimental or not even thought of then. But thanks to persistent research, solid progress has occurred in the fight against cancer. Unlike Rose's parents' diagnoses and my grandmother's, my diagnosis was quick and accurate with state-of-the-art equipment and information that didn't exist almost forty years ago. Still Fear blocked that reality. When I heard the words, "Jean, you have cancer," my thoughts instinctively shifted to the cemetery. I recalled the angel there swathing that ancient headstone. I wondered, would I beat my cancer, or would my headstone be added to the endless rows of others. If I had lingered in those thoughts just a short while longer I might have felt the angel embrace me. And I would have noticed—there were no tears.

CHAPTER 3
The Fat Factor

On New Year's Eve 2010, when the grandfather's clock in my living room struck twelve, I said, "Goodbye crummy decade." The first ten years of the new millennium had been unkind, and I felt relieved to see them go. High hopes and strong ambitions in a century turned fresh had been upset by unpleasant surprises. Both of my parents had died by then leaving me, as Rose would say, an orphan. My writing business and finances suffered along with the sinking economy, and an anxiety disorder that I'd had on and off since my twenties struck with a vengeance and held tight. Life dragged on flat.

I'd also promised myself on that New Year's Eve that I'd eat less and exercise more. But just as I had with most promises to myself, I left it there on the first day of the new year. "I'll start tomorrow," I said. But tomorrow didn't come. Procrastination, laziness, depression. I don't know. Always I put caring for myself aside and especially when it came to the way I ate.

While I was growing up, my mother praised what she called my generosity. I was the kid who willingly allowed everyone to go on ahead, who put herself at the end of the line and quietly accepted that she would be among the last when classmates chose sides. And I shared—everything. I wasn't the stereotypical only child, spoiled, always wanting and getting her way. (I hate that stereotype, incidentally.) Instead, I was quite the opposite, I felt content to be generous, and as Rose once pointed out to me, generous to a fault. I gave endlessly to my friends, and then I filled myself up with food in secret. Food kept me company as I stood alone at the end of the line. Food, my loving and loyal companion. I ate too much and too often, and I did it year after year.

I found out about the obesity risk factor after I got cancer, and truthfully had I known that obesity increases the risk of uterine cancer I probably wouldn't have cared. It's that whole invincible thing again. There's no way cancer is going to get me; cancer only happens to other people. Wouldn't you think I'd have learned my lesson back in the seventies when Grandma Dorothy died? But too many cancer-free years had followed.

I had never worried about damaging my health. My parents had been extraordinarily healthy. Both died when they were old. Mom and Dad never went for checkups, and until their final illnesses neither of them had been seriously sick or hospitalized. In fact, Dad went a solid fifty years without seeing a doctor. I just supposed that I'd be like them and breeze through life healthy to the end. I didn't go to doctors either unless I had to. But when I was in my late fifties, in 2009, and post-menopausal bleeding happened, I absolutely had to. I knew that. Bleeding after menopause is abnormal and requires immediate checking. But, I pushed God's whispers aside, and I climbed into The Hidden Place. I waited there for almost a year.

The reason that I waited was fear, but I used the excuse, and even fooled myself into believing, that I didn't want to inconvenience anyone with my problem, not even God. I imagined that He would make it go away miraculously and whenever He was good and ready. So I went to the end of the line and I waited. And while I waited I ate.

I've had a lifetime of fat. I remember a photograph taken of me at six-months. I'm a chubby baby, bundled for winter, wearing a snowsuit and fuzzy white bonnet. I look like Humpty Dumpty propped up with pillows in Dad's overstuffed easy chair. I'm clueless then that like Humpty Dumpty someday I'll have a great fall. I'll tumble into cancer, and obesity might be part of the cause.

You've heard the saying Eat to live. Don't Live to Eat. In my family that couldn't have been further from the truth. Thick slabs of red meat and mounds of buttery mashed potatoes were staples on our dinner table. Bedtime rarely arrived before a sugary or fatty snack. On Friday nights, my parents and I ate at our favorite restaurants, and dinner ended with pie or ice-cream sundaes. We'd finish our TGIF celebrations by heading downtown and ordering big tubs of popcorn from Mrs. Duchman's popcorn wagon. And on weekends? That's when Mom made pancakes and bacon and eggs for breakfast. Saturday nights were for cheeseburgers and fries delivered to our car by carhops on roller skates at a local drive-in, and on Sunday afternoons we sipped root beer floats on the front porch. My young life was a never-ending sugar and fat feast, and I loved it.

I can't blame my parents for our unhealthy diet. In the fifties and sixties few people worried about sugar and fat. That's when kids grew up on soda pop, slices of white bread slathered with peanut butter, hot dogs, and malted milks. Most elementary schools had a candy store nearby, and Jefferson Elementary where I went to school was no exception. Klein's Confections was next door. Every day, my little friends and I stopped there, and we spent our allowances on candy necklaces, Turkish Taffy, Slo Poke suckers, red wax lips, and Bazooka bubble gum. We left the store carrying small paper bags filled with enough treats to last until bedtime. Consuming sugar and fat back then was as common as saying the Pledge of Allegiance every morning and saluting the flag.

Today, parents are better informed. They know that healthy eating habits begin in childhood. Still, according to the Centers for Disease Control and Prevention, there are nearly three times as many overweight children now than when I was a kid in the fifties and sixties. One in every three children in America is overweight and suffers an increased risk of health problems, including cancer, in adulthood. Many obese kids also suffer emotional problems such as low self-esteem and depression. I know this first hand.

When I was six, I discovered that I was fat. That's when kids in my first grade gym class nicknamed me Plop because of the sound my flabby little body made when I tried to navigate a forward roll on a gym mat.

"Hey, Plop, what's the matter? Are you too fat to tumble? Plop! Plop! Plop!"

I cried to my parents, but they weren't concerned. They told me that as I got taller I would slim down. Mom quipped that the plump American actress Shelley Winters once said, "I'm not overweight. I'm just nine inches too short!"

While we waited for me to grow tall and slim down, Mom bought my clothes in the "chubby" section at the Robert Hall Department Store. Placed atop racks sparsely stocked with little girls' dresses were placards with the word "Chubby." I wore a chubby 6X.

In the fifties, girls wore dresses to school, and pretty dresses were hard to find in my size. Most chubby dresses had garish patterns like you'd see on 1950s curtains and bedspreads. I managed to find one chubby dress at Robert Hall pretty enough to wear for my school's Christmas program. It had a gathered skirt with red and black checks, and a snow-white blouse with puffed sleeves and red trim on its Peter Pan collar. I was thrilled to find a chubby dress that I actually liked, and when I tried it on I felt like a princess. I couldn't wait for the Christmas program so I could show it off.

There was a girl in my first grade class named Martha Ann who loved to make fun of my fatness. (If you're reading this, Martha Ann, I'm sure you grew up to be a very nice person. We should chat over coffee sometime.) She taunted me on the playground with a horrible fat rhyme: "Fatty Fatty two-by-four can't get through the bathroom door—" I can't share the rest. I cringe just thinking about Martha Ann's singsong voice chanting that disgusting rhyme. She was the meanest little girl ever, and while I lived to eat she lived to remind me about just how much I ate.

When the morning of the Christmas program arrived, my mom gave me a pretty, white lacy handkerchief. Handkerchiefs were in style in the fifties. You never saw a little girl whip out a wad of tissue and blow her nose. Instead, she used an embroidered cotton hankie. My dress had no pockets, so Mom safety-pinned the handkerchief to the waistband so if my nose began to trickle during the performance, I could demurely unpin my hankie and daintily dab my leaking nostrils. It was the ladylike thing to do.

My classmates and I waited nervously backstage until it came time to sing our Christmas song. Then, we marched up the stage stairs, tramped onto the wooden stage floor, and sat down in a long, straight line ready to sing "The Twelve Days of Christmas." Our teacher, Mrs. Davis, had assigned each student one of the twelve gifts. Martha Ann had nine ladies dancing, and I had eight maids a'milking. That meant we had to sit next to each other. Not a good thing! The performance rules were simple. Whenever you heard the name of your gift in the song, you stood up and sat down really fast. It couldn't get any easier than that in the first grade. The house lights dimmed, the song started, and very soon my classmates were popping up and down like maniac jacks-in-the-boxes.

On the seventh day of Christmas,
My true love gave to me:
Seven swans a-swimming
Six geese a-laying
Five golden rings
Four calling birds
Three French hens
Two turtle doves and
A partridge in a pear tree.

Eight maids a'milking! It was almost my turn to pop up and sit down.

On the eighth day of Christmas,
My true love gave to me:
Eight maids a-milking . . .

I sprung up, but my dress didn't. Martha Ann had planted her solid little butt firmly on my hankie, and when I popped up, my dress ripped from waistband to hem. Its remnant with the hankie still attached lay flat on the stage floor next to Martha Ann who looked as innocent as one of God's angels.

"Fatty-Fatty, two by four." She said it softly so only I could hear, and then she grinned.

I stood there on stage in front of God and everybody with my underpants showing and the whole world laughing. Mrs. Davis whisked me into the wings where my mother stood waiting. The Great Christmas Rip-Off stayed with me for the rest of first grade. "Hey, Plop. I saw your underpants."

Fat was never good to me and certainly not for me. But even with all the taunting, I clung to it as tightly as I held onto Fear. Fear and Food form a sinister partnership. I'm not making excuses for my obesity, but I grew up in an anxious household, and I allowed food, not Christ, to be my comforter. Fluffernutter sandwiches (Have you had one? A thick layer of chunky peanut butter slathered with marshmallow fluff smooshed between two pieces of white bread), macaroni and cheese, pancakes dripping with syrup, Hershey bars, ice cream; those were my comforters. Ice cream is still my comfort food of choice. Of all fatty and sugary foods, I still find ice cream the most difficult to eat in moderation.

By the end of elementary school I'd slimmed down a little thanks to my sixth grade teacher, a former Marine drill sergeant named Mr. Romanowski. He liked to run our pre-pubescent, out-of-shape bodies all the way from the school building to the children's library a mile away. Sometimes, he made us run laps on the steep oval track at the velodrome, a place near our school where professional bike races happened. I always brought up the rear, and my teacher didn't let me forget it.

"Move it, Fischer! Run! Run! Run! Let's peel off those pounds!"

Winter's cold and snowy weather brought me some relief. I didn't have to participate in Mr. Romanowski's boot camp and listen to him shout anymore about my weight. But he had another equally unpleasant ritual— Friday Dress-Up Day.

Every Friday morning, the girls and the boys had to compete for the titles of Dress-Up King and Dress-Up Queen. The winners got to wear a plastic crown and a sash for the day. (Try that out on today's sixth graders and see what happens.) We girls stood in a line along the blackboards at the front of the room. Then every boy cast his vote aloud, one by one, for the girl he thought was the best dressed that day. With each vote, the best-dressed girl took one step forward leaving the others behind. How damaging is that for a young girl's psyche? After the last boy voted, the girl furthest ahead received the Dress-Up Queen sash and crown. I remained the chubbiest girl in my class, despite Mr. Romanowski's workouts, and at the end of the voting I almost always stood alone against the blackboard wearing a chubby dress from Robert Hall. The inferiority complex I acquired in Mr. Romanowski's class fueled my anxiety, and I ate even more. (Thank you, Mr. Romanowski. Maybe you'd like to join Martha Ann and me for coffee?)

 I slimmed down to almost average weight in middle school and high school, not because I ate less or worried more about how others perceived me, but only because I participated in the schools' marching bands, and I got plenty of exercise. With friends that I'd known since elementary school, I still carried the moniker Plop.

 By the time I went to college, I had horrible self-esteem, and I tried to thwart it with food. I was addicted to overeating. I even volunteered as a delivery service between the residents on my dorm floor and the McDonald's a few blocks away. I'd go room-to-room taking orders and then come back with a box load of hamburgers, cheeseburgers, fries, and Cokes. If someone reneged on his or her order, I'd eat it myself. I can still remember on which day of the week the dorm's cafeteria served a mile-high Reuben sandwich topped with French fried onion rings. I can almost taste the gooey, extra cheese, study-night pizzas that I liked to order from a mom and pop place down the street and The Pig's Trough sundaes at Farrell's Ice Cream Parlor on Downer Avenue. I had become what the bible calls "a glutton" (in today's jargon, a "foodie").

 The word *gluttony* comes from the Latin word *gluttire*. It means to gulp down or swallow. I did my share of both in college, even when I knew that my diet was unhealthy I gulped down gallons of cola and milkshakes, and I swallowed plenty of junk food. In God's eyes, gluttony is a sin. Some Christian religions count it among the Seven Deadly Sins because excessive consumption of food withholds sustenance from the needy. The bible says in Proverbs 23:2, "Put a knife to your throat if you are given to gluttony." Sharp words from King Solomon! In context he was talking about affluence and overindulging to the point of making yourself sick. That's what I did for most of my life: I spent a lot of money on food, and I ate myself sick.

Have you noticed that the bible rarely mentions fat people? I suppose that's because most people walked wherever they went and few had money to spend on indulgences. Only rich folks could afford to buy mass quantities of food and sit around all day scarfing it down. When I imagine biblical kings, queens, and pharaohs, I always picture them obese. In the book of Esther, we discover that King Xerxes gave a banquet that lasted seven days. Feasts like that were common in bible times. Wherever kings and queens lived, a whole lot of eating went on. And, of course, the royals didn't get much exercise. They rode in carriages and chariots. I wonder if their unhealthy habits led to serious health problems including cancer. And if they did have cancer, they probably died from it because none of the treatments existed that we have today.

In the 21st century, we go to fast food restaurants and all-you-can-eat buffets, and we stuff ourselves silly. Then we hop into our cars and head home not thinking about what we've just done to our bodies. If you think about it, not much has changed when it comes to overindulging with food.

As a young woman, I didn't think about the fat cells multiplying inside me. They formed thick, ugly fat layers around my middle, and I remained blissfully unaware that fat increased my risk for certain types of cancers. I certainly didn't consider the effect excess fat might have on estrogen production or how excess estrogen later in life might contribute to cancer, nor did I believe that eating a healthy diet would help me to live longer. I just continued to eat.

Before cancer, if I ate vegetables at all, they were battered, fried, and served in a basket. My weekly diet consisted of a twelve pack of diet cola, high-sodium frozen dinners, a pint or two of ice cream, and take-out meals from fast food restaurants. After cancer, I craved fresh fruit and salads. I'd learned the hard way that healthy eating can preserve good health and that obesity can make us sick.

By the time my post-menopausal bleeding started, I wore X's again, this time a women's 2X. When I finally went to the doctor, I tipped the scale at a whopping 227 pounds! Six weeks later, on the day of my hysterectomy, I'd lost 13 pounds from sheer anxiety. I'm proud to say that now I make better choices. Cancer scared me into getting healthy.

I had only myself to blame for my obesity. Unlike the risk factors of starting my period early and my advancing age, I had control over this one. I knew that the kinds and amounts of food I ate weren't good for my health. Still, I continued a lifetime of unhealthy eating.

Whichever way you look at it, obesity is unhealthy. It affects us physically, emotionally, and spiritually, and it sometimes makes us sick. I am convinced that my excess weight contributed to me getting cancer. So, if you are an overweight woman listen up because I'm ending this chapter with one more boring statistic: According to the American Cancer Society, obese women are three times more likely to develop uterine cancer than women of average weight. If you are overweight, and especially if you are over fifty, please ask your gynecologist about how your weight might increase your risk of getting cancer. Taking action right now could save your life.

CHAPTER 4
Four Barren Women

Don was a sweet boy whom I knew in ninth grade. We met in the marching band where I played the piccolo and Don played the tuba. We lived in adjoining neighborhoods, and always I was the one running to catch up with Don so we could walk home from school together. I didn't know if he liked me the same way that I liked him; I wished that he were my boyfriend. Sometimes, awkward moments slipped into our walks, times when neither of us spoke and silence grew thick with anticipation.

I might have suspected that Don was interested in more than friendship when he began waiting for me at the door when school let out. One day, he suggested that we team up to perform a piccolo and tuba duet at the school's spring concert. Naivety kept me from understanding the subtle elements of courtship. His suggestion meant that if I agreed to the duet, we'd be spending more time together. Back in the sixties, it took a boy a while to gather enough courage to ask a girl on a date. I had never been on a date, and I don't think that Don had either.

On the way home from school one day, Don became extraordinarily quiet. We were almost to my house when he stopped and grabbed my forearm.

"Let's just face it, Jean," he said. "I like you and you like me, and two people who like each other belong together. Will you wear my ring?"

Of course, Don didn't mean an engagement ring. Since he wasn't yet a senior he didn't have a high school ring, so what he offered me was his middle school graduation ring. It had a purple plastic "stone" with a small bronze-colored tiger's head glued to it, also plastic. Etched into the ring's band were the words *Washington Wildcats*. Back then, if a girl accepted a guy's class ring, she wrapped its band in angora yarn and wore it around her neck on a chain. It meant that she was going steady.

"Will you?" he asked again.

Don had skipped right over suggesting that we have ice cream at the Dutch Maid on the way home from school or catch a Saturday afternoon matinee at the Orpheum Theater. He went straight to going steady! I didn't know what to do. I wanted to accept his ring, but I decided that Don wouldn't be good enough for my dad, nor would I be good enough for Don. So I ran home leaving the poor boy standing there. For the rest of high school, I tried my best to ignore him. Whenever he tried to be nice to me, I responded with rudeness. I felt embarrassed by my behavior, but my fear of intimacy, rejection, and of not being good enough was so intense that I had to push Don away. That high school experience set a lifelong pattern. There would be other men in my life left standing bewildered while Fear made me run for safety.

When I became old enough to get married, I chose to be single. I believed in marriage before children, so I also set myself up to be childless. Little did I know that the choices I made then would increase my risk of getting cancer later in life. (In 2012, the American Cancer Society reported that women who have never been pregnant are at a higher risk of getting uterine cancer.)

Fear served as the architect of my behavior toward men. It made me afraid to become involved in a serious relationship, afraid that eventually he would see that I wasn't worthy of him, and then he would leave me. This "he" was a faceless entity, a wonderful, blameless man who would love me and think of me as sweet and loveable but then find out who I really was. He would regret the horrible mess that he'd gotten himself into. How is that for low self-esteem?

Fear kept me from bringing my dates home to meet my

parents. My dad expected perfection from me, and I knew that he'd find imperfection in any man that I chose. This is the reason that I bolted from Don and other men in my life. I believed that no one I dated could ever meet Dad's high expectations, and I didn't want to put any man through the scrutiny. So, I remained single.

My friends tell me that my brain works in odd ways. But what they find odd is normal for me. When I'm idle, my head swims with what I call "snapshots." These brief glimpses transcend time and last split seconds. In an instant, I might remember sitting in the car yesterday waiting for a red light, then flash to roller-skating when I was eight, then imagine someone, someplace, or something from a book I've read. Usually these snapshots go by and I hardly notice, but sometimes one catches my attention and makes me wonder. Shortly after my cancer diagnosis, I had a snapshot of three women from the bible, Rebekah, Elizabeth and Michal.

I caught a fleeting glimpse of them standing arm-in-arm. I imagined Rebekah young and beautiful and Elizabeth old and haggard. Between them stood Michal, a middle-aged woman, maybe in her 50's, her identity veiled by the striking clarity and difference of the others. I had learned about these three in a bible study about barren women. I don't like that word *barren*. Proverbs 30:16 calls a barren womb "a grave, a land which is never satisfied." How bleak is that? Yet, it's so true for women who want to have children but can't. Rebekah, Elizabeth, and Michal were all barren—they were childless.

Lovely Rebekah, Isaac's wife, struggled with infertility. For twenty years this couple patiently asked God for a child. When God's answer finally came, it was yes. Did the symptoms of pregnancy confuse Rebekah? Years of infertility diminished the hope that she could become pregnant. Some bible scholars estimate Rebekah's age when she married Isaac at around fourteen, so at age thirty-four pregnancy was certainly possible but not probable given that she and Isaac had been trying unsuccessfully for two decades to have children. The bible says in Genesis 25:22 that when Rebekah felt strange sensations inside her uterus she went to God and said, "Why is this happening to me?" Most likely, these physical sensations made her afraid. After years of having a period, suddenly it stopped. Her stomach began to swell a bit, and she sensed something strange going on inside her. I doubt that the word *cancer* existed back then, but Rebekah must have worried that instead of a pregnancy, something might be wrong "down there." And, of course, there were no gynecologists, ultrasounds, or pregnancy tests to confirm her suspicion. Her mind rested only when God told her that she was indeed pregnant. Months later, Rebekah gave birth to twin boys, Jacob and Esau.

Worried that something might be wrong down there; that's how I identified with Rebekah. Odd physical changes inside my body that didn't feel right finally sent me searching for answers.

When we don't feel well and expect the worst, we ask God, "Why is this happening to me?" I asked Him that question, Rebekah asked it, and so did our second childless woman, Elizabeth.

Elizabeth was married to the priest named Zecharias. In my snapshot I saw her in stark contrast to Rebekah. The old, wrinkled, sagging skin on Elizabeth's face reminded me of how Grandma Lily had looked in her old age.

Like Rebekah and Isaac, Elizabeth and Zacharias sent up plenty of prayers asking God for children, and nearing the end of their years they received God's answer, another yes. This time, the angel Gabriel appeared to Zacharias and said, "Do not be afraid, Zecharias; your prayer has been heard. Your wife Elizabeth will bear you a son."

The problem here is that this couple was old. The bible doesn't tell us how old, but by the time Gabriel showed up and gave Zacharias the good news, Zacharias must have already given up the hope of having a child. Most likely, he and Elizabeth hadn't prayed in that regard for a long time. Still, God had heard Zacharias' prayer, and He answered it in His own perfect time.

Zacharias said to Gabriel, ""How can I be sure of this? I am an old man and my wife is well along in years. "

In other words, Zacharias said to Gabriel, "Get out of town! There's no way Elizabeth is going to have a baby. Not at her age."

Remember, I've told you how my brain goes numb when I face a crisis? Well, Zacharias went numb, too. Literally, he was struck silent. Gabriel rendered him unable to speak until Elizabeth's baby was born. Why? Because Zacharias doubted the truth. And who wouldn't after so many years without an answer to prayer?

How did Elizabeth react to all of this? At her age surely she was post-menopausal. To become pregnant, her periods must have started again. Did she worry about the bleeding? Did she think, as Rebekah must have, that something was wrong down there? Did she cry out to God, "What is happening to me?" This is the place where I connect with Elizabeth. We were both in menopause.

My menopause was late, another risk factor for uterine cancer. In my mid-fifties, I went almost a year without having a period, and then it started again. Menopause can be confusing because so much about a woman's body changes so quickly. After a while, weird feelings and subtle changes become normal; you expect them. So, when my period started after eleven months, I convinced myself that it was a natural part of menopause. It wasn't until I began spotting at random that I asked God, "What's going on? Why is this happening to me?"

I wonder how women in Elizabeth's time fought the hot flashes, insomnia, and other unpleasant side effects of menopause. Perhaps with potions and herbs or not at all. Today, some menopausal women choose hormone replacement therapy. It was offered to me, but I rejected it.

Hormone therapy is something that women should discuss with their doctors and weigh carefully. There are both benefits of this treatment and risks. When I faced cancer, I read on the American Cancer Society website that hormone replacement therapy, either estrogen replacement therapy (ERT) or combined hormone replacement therapy (HRT), might increase a woman's chances of getting uterine cancer. I wasn't aware of this risk, and I am grateful that I decided against those treatments. This turned out to be a blessing, one less risk factor for my growing list.

Although Zacharias was speechless, he must have communicated to Elizabeth what Gabriel said and reassured her that she would be fine. Elizabeth felt thrilled about her pregnancy. We know this because in Luke 1:25, she says, "The Lord has done this for me. In these days he has shown his favor and taken away my disgrace among the people."

What did Elizabeth mean by her disgrace?

Her disgrace was barrenness, the inability to have a child. In Elizabeth's time, women were expected to be chaste before marriage and then bear children, especially an heir, a son. Elizabeth was infertile. She thought of herself as less of a woman because of it, and others thought less of her, too. Elizabeth's story ends well, though. She carried her baby boy full term, a healthy boy who grew up to be John the Baptist, a man with great significance in the life of Christ.

I can empathize with Elizabeth's feelings of disgrace. In my childbearing years, I watched most of my girlfriends get married and have children. When I held their babies, I felt aware of that missing piece in my life. I had no babies of my own to hold, and while *disgrace* is too strong a word for what I felt, I did feel inadequate and less than equal to my friends who were mothers. I still feel that way when I see my friends with their grandchildren. Because I didn't raise children, I don't understand the nuances in all the stages that they go through. It limits what I'm able to share with friends who are mothers and grandmothers. I can't say to them, "Oh, my Freddie did that, too." There's a chasm that can't be bridged. Do they feel sorry for me or think of me as less of a woman because I am childless? I don't know. I think some of them might.

The third childless woman in my snapshot, Michal, was the daughter of King Saul. Michal loved a popular guy named David. Who wouldn't love David? He'd killed the giant, Goliath, which made him a celebrity. He was strong and handsome and also a musician. What more could a girl ask for?

In 1 Samuel 18:27, we read that King Saul gave Michal to David to be his wife. That's what dads did in biblical times, they chose a mate for their daughters and then literally they gave their daughters away, often to men they didn't love. Michal was lucky that her dad really liked David and wanted her to marry him. Later though, King Saul turned against his son-in-law. And what caused the rift? Fear. King Saul wasn't at all happy that God loved David and favored him. As David became more powerful and well liked among the people, Michal's dad saw him as a threat, and that's where the drama begins.

King Saul made a plan to have David killed. This left Michal to choose between her father and her husband. Bravely, she chose David. When the king's men came to assassinate David, Michal helped him escape out a window. Then she put an idol, a fake David, into their bed, and she lied to the assassins saying that David was sick. David was long gone by then, saved by his wife's quick thinking.

You won't believe what happened next. David didn't come home for a good long while, and after he did come back, their marriage went sour. Eventually they split up. 2 Samuel 6:23 tells us that Michal never had children. Poor Michal. She falls for this hunky guy, David, and then he rejects her and her life falls apart. She ends up feeling bitter toward David and possibly bitter toward God.

I identify most with Michal, the veiled woman-in-the-middle in my snapshot. We both had powerful, disapproving dads. I wonder if she regretted telling her father that she loved David. Did she wish that she had remained single and escaped King Saul's disapproval? When David left her, did she think he left because she wasn't good enough? Like me, did she grieve the loss of babies not born, not even conceived?

Childless women often grieve when their ability to have children ends, especially when the end comes from a hysterectomy. For those who haven't gone through menopause yet it's especially hard.

My friend, Kelli, had severe endometriosis that required a hysterectomy the year she turned forty. Like Rebekah's story, God's answer to Kelli's endless praying for a child came after she and John were married twenty years. This time God said no. Kelli and her husband had tried everything to have children, and when faced with a hysterectomy, Kelli felt almost unbearable grief knowing that her chances of getting pregnant were over. She blamed herself.

"I feel like I've failed," she confided in me. "I've let John down and our parents, too. They'll never have grandchildren."

Now, at almost sixty-years old, Kelli still grieves for the child she never had. She tells me that it's hard seeing her friends become grandmothers. She calculates the age of her imagined son or daughter and thinks about how life might be different if she were a mother. Kelli worries, too, about who will care for her and John in their old age. Both are only children, and neither has any close family members left.

"I trust that God exists and that He has a plan for us," Kelli tells me, "But still, I ask Him why."

I asked God why, too. I grieved when I learned that a hysterectomy was the cure for my uterine cancer. My grief came from the choices I'd made earlier in my life beginning with that day that I'd left Don standing alone on the sidewalk. I hadn't intended to remain single and childless. As the years slipped by, I figured that sooner or later I would find a way to push Fear aside and allow that faceless "he" into my life. But it never happened. I had even planned my wedding the summer before I left for college.

I wasn't dating anyone then, but I've always been the kind of person who plans ahead. I felt sure that in a few years marriage would be a probability. So, one warm July night, I got out my journal and a pencil, and with the aid of a bride's magazine. I began putting together the pieces of my wedding puzzle.

I remember that Cheryl Tiegs was on the magazine's cover. She wore a sleek satin gown with a long train and an empire waist. The dress's lavishly decorated bodice had clear beads in a delicate floral pattern. A pillbox hat with a poufy nylon veil sat atop Cheryl's wavy, shoulder-length hair. Oh, how I wanted to be her! As I paged through the magazine's abundant pictures of bridesmaid dresses, beauty articles, wedding venues, and honeymoon destinations, my brain spun with wonderful ideas.

I jotted down that my intimate wedding would happen in the small brick chapel on the grounds of an archaic convent in my hometown. The chapel overlooked Lake Michigan, one of my favorite spots. In my journal, I added and underlined the words <u>September on a starry, moonlit night</u>. Guests would enter the chapel at dusk and find it softly lit by hundreds of glowing candles. Then as dusk turned to darkness and a string quartet played the "Wedding March," I'd walk down the aisle bathed in candlelight following bridesmaids dressed in pastel shades of autumn.

Sounds lovely, doesn't it? But if I'd looked closely at my fantasy wedding, I would have noticed a smudge of red lipstick on my gleaming white teeth. Imperfection. I had forgotten two essential pieces of the wedding puzzle, the groom and my dad. For my wedding to become a reality, I needed to find a groom and connect his puzzle piece with my father's. Without that connection, there would be no wedding and I'd have no children. I put the puzzle aside that day, and I never went back to complete it.

It seems cruel that childlessness might bring a woman one step closer to cancer. But then, Jesus did say in John 16:33. "In this world you will have trouble."

The three barren women in my snapshot, Rebekah, Elizabeth, and Michal, all had trouble. And so did I. Had the snapshot remained in my head just a little while longer, I might have seen a fourth barren women there—me—the childless woman with cancer.

Sometimes, God gives us what we ask for in prayer, and other times He has a different plan, a good plan that works things out for His glory. In Isaiah 54:5, God has a message for barren women. He says, "For your maker is your husband—the Lord Almighty is his name—the Holy One of Israel is your Redeemer; he is called God of all the earth."

As I let my cancer diagnosis soak in, I allowed myself to say the word *cancer*. I said it, and I could not pretend that it was separate from me. So, I pushed it into The Hidden Place and I turned my thoughts to how I would handle this unbelievable thing that was happening to me.

I decided that I would do what Elizabeth and Rebekah had done. I would rely on my Heavenly Husband for help. I knelt down, and I prayed: "Even though I walk through the Valley of the Shadow of Death, I will fear no evil, for You are with me."

Reader's Notes—Part One

Use this page to write your thoughts and concerns about cancer's risk factors.

Part Two – Living Through Cancer

CHAPTER 5
Blind Man's Bluff

I love the line in "Fiddler on the Roof" where Yente, the gossipy village matchmaker says to nineteen-year-old Tzeitel, "Tzeitel, if God lived on Earth, people would break His windows."

Have you ever been so mad at God that you wanted to break His windows? Only believers can answer yes. Atheists can't rant at God because there is no God to rant at, and when agnostics get angry they may or may not cry out to a god who might or might not hear them. I think of the French philosopher Ernest Renen's The Prayer of the Agnostic: "O God, if there is a God, save my soul if I have a soul."

I can't imagine facing a crisis like cancer without a steadfast belief in God. Even in non-believing hearts there must be a gently tugging primal intuition that life is a gift that cannot be revoked.

In the days before my cancer surgery, I went online to a website where women meet to discuss their hysterectomies. One woman wrote about the rage she felt when her doctor offered surgery as the only treatment for her endometrial cancer. She hadn't fit any of the risk factors. She was married and young enough to become pregnant. The woman and her husband had one child, and they were trying for another. "At first, I was angry with my uterus," she wrote. "But then, I realized that it had been faithful to me. Each month, it prepared itself hoping that it would have the chance to nurture new life. I owe all of my gratitude to my uterus. My uterus never let me down. It was the one who kept hope alive. The real villain in all of this and the one that I'm angry with is God."

I find it interesting that this woman personified her uterus and imagined that it had the ability to hope and the power to be faithful. Whether she was an agnostic or a believer I don't know, but that she mentions God leads me to think that on some level she believes in Him. Her blame had to go somewhere, and she put it squarely on God. She was all set to pick up a rock and break His windows. A cancer diagnosis does that to some people. It makes them want to smash God's windows.

In her 1969 book *On Death and Dying*, Doctor Elizabeth Kübler-Ross outlined five stages that most people go through when they face an overwhelming crisis like cancer. You might know them as The Five Stages of Grief. The first stage is Denial. Surely God, You wouldn't let this happen to me. After Denial comes Anger. This is the stage where you want to smash God's windows. You scream, *"God, why?!"* Then after you've ranted at God for a while, you Bargain with Him. "I'll do anything, God, if only you make this cancer go away." And when the cancer doesn't go away, Depression comes, that hollow, sinking hopelessness that thrusts you into the valley where tears fall. Then you cry out, "God, where are you? And even "God, ARE you?" Finally, when you can't deny, rant, bargain, or cry anymore, you reach the final stage, Acceptance. Cancer is the hand that you were dealt. This is what God has decided to allow into your life. Notice that I said, "allow". God does not cause bad things to happen to us, but He allows them to happen for His perfect reasons, whether or not we like or understand them.

When the late Tony Snow, Press Secretary in the George W. Bush administration, resigned his job in 2007, he had recently learned that his colon cancer recurred and had spread to his abdomen. In an essay for Christianity Today, published shortly before he resigned, Snow wrote about cancer's unexpected blessings: "We shouldn't spend too much time trying to answer the why questions: Why me? Why must people suffer? Why can't someone else get sick? We can't answer such things, and the questions themselves often are designed more to express our anguish than to solicit an answer." He went on to suggest that Christianity isn't "doughy, passive, pious, and soft," but rather filled with "thrills, boldness, danger, shocks, reversals, triumphs, and epiphanies. The mere thought of death somehow makes every blessing vivid, every happiness more luminous and intense."

Wow, that's acceptance.

Earlier, I explained to you how my family responded when Cancer beat Grandma Dorothy, and I told you about the scars Rose bore after Cancer killed her parents. Everyone who has a close relationship with Cancer goes through some of the five stages of grief, but not necessarily in a timely way nor in the order set by Kübler-Ross. Some get stuck in denial, anger, bargaining, or depression, and they might remain there forever. The lucky ones make it through to acceptance.

My friend Linda is in the middle of a cancer battle. She's not the one who is sick, but instead her 78-year old mother. For much of her adult life, Linda has guided her parents through an array of illnesses beginning with her mother's breast cancer more than twenty years ago. I can't remember a time since then when Linda didn't have an issue with her parents' failing health: a degenerative eye disease, a seriously complicated heart surgery, diabetes, an ulcerated ankle too stubborn to heal. Now Linda's mom has cancer again, and this time it's terminal.

Linda works fulltime at a business more than an hour away from home. Still, she makes time to take her mom to all her chemotherapy and other doctors' appointments. She cleans her parents' house, prepares their meals, runs errands for them, and stops at their house to check on them in the morning before she goes to work and then again at the end of her work day. In my opinion, Linda qualifies for sainthood. There is no spouse or significant other in Linda's life to help out with daily tasks. Like me, Linda never married and she has no children. Her siblings leave most of the caretaking to her.

Linda is well beyond the "this can't be happening to me" stage. She's ready to break God's windows. A spiritual, bible-reading Christian, Linda sees her faith seeping away one drop at a time. Years of unanswered prayers leave her unable to pray. She's angry with God. Really angry with Him! She's angry with herself, too, for losing her faith.

"I feel ugly," she tells me.

"Ugly" meaning "nasty." Linda's patience is gone. Her temper is short. Her mood is indeed ugly. I worry about her because I've been there. I know how ugliness feels. When you desert God and lose faith in Him, then ugliness moves in, and its name is Satan.

I deserted God shortly after I became a confirmed member of the church. Confirmation is a rite where baptized individuals make a public affirmation of their faith. In my church confirmation happened the year kids turned thirteen.

To prepare for the rite of confirmation, I attended classes to learn about God, faith, and the church. Then, when Confirmation Sunday arrived, my classmates and I dressed in long, white robes and we stood in front of the congregation ready to confirm our faith.

The pastor set up a microphone in the church's center aisle, and each candidate recited a memorized scripture verse and told why he or she believed in God. When we were through, the pastor turned to us and asked, "As members of Christ's universal church, will you be loyal to the Methodist Church and do all in your power to strengthen its ministries?"

"I will," we answered in unison.

"And as members of this congregation, will you faithfully participate in its ministries by your prayers, your presence, your gifts, and your service?"

"I will," we answered again.

Then we knelt in a straight row in front of the altar so the pastor could offer us our first communion.

I wore high heels that Sunday and nylon stockings too, my first time for both. As I'd gotten dressed that morning, I felt so grown up slipping on each stocking, gently rolling its top up to mid-thigh, then fastening it to my new, lacy garter belt. And my two-inch white heels looked trés chic, even if they did make me wobbly when I walked.

At the pastor's command, I knelt, and I prayed. I accepted a small piece of cubed white bread from the brass plate the pastor held before me. Then I washed the bread down with a swallow of grape juice from a tiny plastic cup. With our confirmation and first communion over, we stood up. Everyone except me.

The heel of my right shoe caught in the hem of my robe, and I tumbled backward in a somersault that would have made my first-grade gym class proud. I backslid into the microphone. It collapsed just missing sour Mrs. Petzke who always sat at the end of the front row. Mortified, I picked up my shoe, which had come off during the fall, and I stood facing the parishioners.

Ours was a pious German Methodist church, and no one dared laugh in God's house. I was grateful for that. But a sea of stone-cold faces glared at me. Where was all that love that we'd learned about in confirmation class? God is love. God's people help each other. God's people—they love, love, love! I think in that single embarrassing moment ugliness crept in. Where was the compassion of other Christians? My mother and Grandma Lily rushed to my aid, but no one else.

Now, I'm not saying that this was the only reason I deserted God. A disagreement, not long after my confirmation, between the pastor and some church members sent my family searching for a new church home. Sadly, we never found one. We visited a few and stayed a while, but eventually we stopped going to church altogether. We remained faithful to God, but He came to our house instead of us going to His.

In the following years, I thought very little about my Christian faith. When Grandma Dorothy was in surgery I got on my knees and prayed like an agnostic.

"Oh, God, if you really exist and if you are able, please make my grandma well again. Thank you very much. Amen."

You already know God's answer.

When Grandma Dorothy died, instead of wanting to smash God's windows I planted myself in denial and retreated to The

Hidden Place. I denied the certainty of God's existence. How can you be mad at something when you're reasonably sure that it doesn't exist? I fell into a trap that snares many of us: if God is real and He is good, then why do bad things happen?

Ugliness thrives on that question. Ugliness says, "It's because there is no God," or "It's because God isn't involved in our lives anymore." Ugliness' best argument is, "It's because God doesn't love you. You are such a bad and undeserving person that God is punishing you."

I listened to Ugliness. I decided that God is not absolute, and I stayed in that cynical stage for almost a decade.

Rose told me once that she imagined Satan as someone who looked like a stuffy, British stage actor wearing a red, velvet smoking jacket. She called him Neville B. Goodenov. Rose imagined Neville sitting next to her on the sofa, puffing on a cigarette in a long, black-lacquered holder. In a heavy British accent Neville would say to her, "My dear, you'll never be good enough." Imagining this Neville character helped Rose put Satan in perspective.

"It's easier to accept the concept of a fatheaded Neville," she said, "than a manipulative, evil spirit from hell."

Neville must have grown tired of Rose, because he showed up at my house about ten years after Grandma Dorothy died. He was far more than fatheaded. He vacationed in my soul all expenses paid, and he brought along plenty of baggage.

I tried my best to be a good host, but I could never do enough for Neville. He berated me until I felt so worthless that I found it almost impossible to get out of bed in the morning. Every day, he sat there on my sofa, puffing on his cigarette, muttering about my faults. He made me cry. I begged him to be better to me, but Neville didn't care. He lived the good life in my depressed soul as if it were a penthouse suite in the Upper East Side of Manhattan.

I was thirty-three years old, still lost inside of myself and hunting for answers, stuck in agnosticism, and Neville owned me. I was his servant instead of a servant to Christ. I longed for something that would free me from this bondage, but as I traveled my inner roads I found nothing.

When I searched deeper into myself, I pulled away from

family members and friends until I sabotaged all of my close relationships. Finally, there was just Neville and me—and that's exactly how he wanted it.

I slipped into a routine that lasted for months. When I came home from work, I changed into sweat pants and a tee shirt, and I lay on the sofa where I listened to Neville criticize me until it was time for bed. I rarely ate, and when I did it wasn't much. Neville said that I wasn't worth a decent meal. I didn't read, watch television, or go out of the house. I just lay there in a living room filled with Neville's stale cigarette smoke, waiting for the late afternoon sun to wither into darkness.

I lost a lot of weight. "You look great, Jean," my co-workers said. But I didn't want to hear it. Neville told me the truth. I didn't look great. I looked fat and ugly. I believed him. Shedding the excess pounds made me feel naked and defenseless. Even worse, it threatened to shout the secret of my depression to the world, a secret that I didn't want anyone to know.

Loneliness swallowed me up, and I ached to be free from Neville for good.

In the movie Forrest Gump, the character Lieutenant Daniel Taylor says to Forrest, "Have you found Jesus yet, Gump"?

Forrest answers him, "I didn't know I was supposed to be looking for him, sir."

I didn't know that I was supposed to be looking for Jesus either, and I certainly didn't expect to find Him deep in the valley of my depression. Still, that's where He waited for me—Jesus—silently working in the background carrying out His perfect plan, —Jesus— working out all things for good.

Early one morning, I took a walk along the Lake Michigan shore. The gloomy sky promised rain as seagulls circled above me and waves rolled toward me, vast and unpredictable. I wandered along a path on a windy bluff trying to decide whether I wanted to live with Neville or die to be rid of him.

Many years earlier, Mrs. Patterson, a neighbor when I was growing up, decided to die rather than to live with her Neville. Before dawn one summer morning, she walked straight into Lake Michigan and kept on walking. When I stood there on the bluff, I wondered if Mrs. Patterson believed in God or was she an agnostic like me. Did she walk into heaven, or did she walk into nothingness?

I like these words attributed to the poet, Robert Frost: "Don't be an agnostic—be something!" Standing there on the bluff, I felt that gentle tugging, primal intuition that I wrote about earlier in this chapter. Agnostic wasn't working for me. I wanted to be something.

I struggled to remember and say the words of a prayer that I hadn't prayed since I was thirteen:

"Our Father, who art in Heaven, hallowed be thy name. Thy kingdom come; thy will be done, on earth as it is in Heaven. Give us this day our daily bread, and forgive us our trespasses as we forgive those who trespass against us. And lead us not into temptation, but deliver us from evil. For thine is the kingdom, and the power and the glory forever.

Jesus," I whispered, ending my prayer. "I need you."

I offered the prayer in desperation, hungry to connect with God, to believe that He was, and that He loved me enough to save my life.

Words tumbled into my head then, powerful, authoritative words.

"Look out at the water, and the sun shall shine upon you."

Could my mind be playing tricks on me? My thoughts didn't sound like that. I wouldn't say to myself, "The sun shall shine upon you." I looked out at the horizon and I saw a patch of blue in the harsh, gray sky. Had it been there all along? Then the sun broke through casting iridescent beams onto the lake. The water appeared to be drawing up and into the clouds, and I heard God's voice speak to my heart.

"Hold nothing with more love than you have for Me."

Wow! God was speaking to me. I had blindly denied His existence, but suddenly THERE HE WAS! On the bluff that day, I gave my whole self to Jesus. He came into my heart, and my depression changed to acceptance.

The road to acceptance is never paved, narrow, and straight. It is long, dirty, and littered with potholes and detours. But I had begun walking down Acceptance Road. I accepted the bad things that had happened to me. I accepted whatever my future held. I accepted that God was and is. The sweetness of my Redeemer's voice drowned Neville's condemning whispers, and my soul no longer allowed him the four-star accommodations that he preferred. Neville packed his bags, and he left.

Years later when my doctor told me that I had uterine cancer, I repeated the words aloud, soft and slow, "I have cancer." I might have ranted at God then and wanted to break His windows. I might have been so overwhelmed by the journey that lay ahead of me that I turned away from God. (Neville would have loved that.) But instead, I turned toward my Heavenly Father, and I asked Him to walk with me.

The psychologist David Seabury said, "Your desires and true beliefs have a way of playing blind man's bluff. You must corner the inner facts."

The inner facts hold the truth that God pursues us. He desires for us to find Him. He continuously works His plan for each of us. Our problem is that it takes a lifetime for Him to bring His plan to fruition, and patience doesn't come easy for us humans. When we become impatient, ugliness takes hold and threatens to steal our faith.

Remember Rebekah and Elizabeth? God knew the perfect time for their babies to arrive—when they least expected. That's how God often works. He does the unexpected. He brings good and allows not so good events into our lives, all of it leading to the end of His plan, the day when He's finished with us here on Earth.

I know now that God began preparing me for cancer when I met Him on the bluff that morning. He made me ready to grow in Him and learn to accept the bad things with the good.

When I heard my cancer diagnosis, I remembered Psalm 37:7-9. "Be still before the Lord and wait patiently for him . . . Refrain from anger and turn from wrath; do not fret—it leads only to evil. For evil men will be cut off, but those who hope in the Lord will inherit the land."

So instead of deciding to smash God's windows, I made the decision to hope.

CHAPTER 6
Menopausal Mystery

A few years ago, I decided to freshen my journalism writing skills by taking a night class at a local college. I was the oldest student in the class, and I tried desperately to fit in with my younger classmates. They accepted me, and I felt like one of the gang until one dreadful night when my face suddenly turned scarlet and I broke out in a dripping sweat. I hoped that no one would notice.

"Are you okay," said twenty-something Jenn who sat next to me.

"Yeah," I said swiping my forehead with a soggy tissue.

"Are you sure?" she asked again, this time loud enough for others to hear.

All eyes turned toward me. "It's just a hot flash," I confessed to a sea of blank stares. What could I say to these kids that would help them to understand? "You know," I tried. "Like you read about in the AARP newsletters."

Jenn looked relieved. "Oh," she said. "My grandma gets those."

Wonderful.

The instructor was giving a lecture on why tabloid articles are not good writing, and at that moment I felt like I could end up the topic of one of those articles: MIDDLE-AGED WOMAN SELF-

COMBUSTS IN CLASSROOM.

I read a story in a tabloid about a woman who disintegrated in her home. Nothing else burned, just her. And yes, the story had a picture. Imagine The Wizard of Oz, the part where The Wicked Witch of the West melts and only her hat and shoes are left. It was like that. Investigators found the woman's ashy form on her living room floor. Her shoes, an almost empty beer can, and a trashy romance novel lay nearby in perfect condition, not even singed. Cause of death: spontaneous human combustion, a very rare phenomenon in which a chemical reaction in the body makes it burst spontaneously into flames. Poof! In a flash you're gone.

I told my cousin's son, Jack, about it. He used to be a firefighter.

"There's no way!" Jack said. "That's totally impossible."

"No, it's not!" I argued. "I have proof. It's almost happened to me—a bunch of times."

Obviously, Jack didn't understand about menopausal women and hot flashes, nor did he believe that everything you read in tabloids is true.

Some women's hot flashes begin at the base of the neck and slowly creep upward. Their faces burn, sweat streams down, their hair falls limp and damp. But my hot flashes began differently. Mine started deep inside my body and radiated outward. I felt as if I were in a microwave oven cooking from the inside out. No red face, no sweating. If you looked at me, you wouldn't have a clue that in seconds I might disintegrate into a pile of ashes right before your very eyes. But it was after that initial inner burning that my hot flash burst through my skin sending an abrupt fiery glow to my face and sweat gushing from my pores. Not a pretty sight and frightening to people like Jenn who had never witnessed such a thing.

Hot flashes, like most symptoms of menopause, are often unpredictable. In fact, the whole idea of menopause is wishy-washy.

Most women use *menopause* as a catchall word for symptoms leading up to the day when their periods stop forever. But according to the Mayo Clinic, menopause is when a woman's period ends permanently and she is no longer fertile. If she has gone a full year without a period, then most likely she has reached menopause. Technically, a woman is in menopause for just that split second when her period shuts off for good. And only God knows when that is. After that, she's called "postmenopausal."

That transitional stage mistakenly called "menopause," the stage where women get hot flashes, night sweats, mood swings, and insomnia is really perimenopause. The length of it varies from woman to woman, but some women ride the perimenopause roller coaster for five years or more before they hit that magic twelve-month bull's-eye. Along the way, their periods might become irregular. Am I there yet, a woman might wonder. She begins counting . . . nine months, ten months, eleven months. Then if her period starts up again, she has to start counting all over again.

My perimenopause began in my forties and with a racing heart. Occasionally, my heart would flutter for several minutes and then return to its normal rhythm. Of course this worried me. After a while, I reluctantly made an appointment with my family doctor. He examined me and ordered blood work. Everything came back fine.

"I think you're just stressed out," he said. "Learn to relax. Don't worry so much."

He took out his prescription pad and wanted to prescribe a tranquilizer, but I refused.

"Listen, " I said. "I know that my heart is doing weird things, and I want to know why."

So, he referred me to a cardiologist, and one week later I had a stress test and an echocardiogram. Again, everything looked fine. The cardiologist agreed with my doctor.

"It's just stress," he said. "Let's try a mild tranquilizer."

Again, I refused.

These random episodes of heart racing continued on for several months. Then, one day, Oprah Winfrey did a show about menopause. Her featured guest, a woman doctor, mentioned that one of her perimenopause symptoms had been a racing heart.

"Me, too!" said Oprah.

They went on to discuss how hormonal changes can contribute to a rapid heartbeat. The guest said that some doctors miss the menopause connection and attribute the arrhythmia to stress.

That sounded familiar.

I had nothing against male doctors, but when it came to menopause, I believed that a woman doctor might be more empathetic. So, I decided to find a woman doctor whom I could trust. After asking around, I found one with a great reputation for helping with "the change." Doctor P. examined me, reviewed my records, and said that I was in perimenopause. My hormones were raging just like they had when I was eleven and got my first period.

"We can start you on birth control pills," Doctor P. suggested. "They'll regulate your body's estrogen and progesterone levels and help with perimenopause symptoms like hot flashes, sleep problems, and depression."

"And the heart flutters?" I wondered.

"Those should stop, too," she said. "Once your hormones settle down."

Doctor P. pointed out the risks of taking the birth control pill: heart attack, stroke, breast cancer . . . .

"But I wouldn't worry too much about it," she said. "You'll be fine."

I wanted a little time to think about it. I told her that I'd weigh the pros and cons and let her know my decision.

The hormone-balancing act is a risky one. Some of the research shows that using oral contraceptives might increase the risk of breast cancer; however, research also shows that oral contraceptives can decrease the risk of uterine cancer. I can't remember if Doctor P. told me this. If she did, uterine cancer meant nothing to me then. No one talked about it. But breast cancer? That was everywhere in the media, and it was scary.

I've never been one to take medicine unless I seriously need it, so I chose not to use birth control pills. If I had decided to take them, only God knows if it might have prevented my uterine cancer.

As I aged, the heart fluttering stopped, but the hot flashes and night sweats grew worse. Then Doctor P. suggested estrogen replacement therapy (ERT). I decided against that, too. Again, the research shows that taking estrogen alone for many years as menopausal hormone therapy can increase the risk of uterine cancer. Too much estrogen might cause cells in the uterus to grow abnormally and become cancerous. Every woman has to weigh the pros and cons and decide what's best for her, but I believe that God put it in my heart back then to say no to hormone therapy. In doing so, I might have avoided another uterine cancer risk.

According to Pamela Boggs, former Director of Education and Development at the North American Menopause Society, every woman's menopause experience is unique. That's where the confusion comes. People experience symptoms at different times.

My perimenopause was indeed unique and also confusing. I was fifty-six before I skipped a period. Until then, I had been menstruating normally. The average age a woman has her last period is fifty-one. So, I was well beyond average. I wasn't concerned, though, because I had learned with perimenopause to expect the unexpected. I skipped a month, then I was regular again for several months, then I skipped a month again. I knew that I was nearing menopause, and I presumed that soon my period would stop altogether. It did. I counted the months to eleven. Then I started bleeding again, this time very light and lasting only a few days. I wasn't too worried about the light, erratic spotting. It seemed to cycle every twenty-eight days or so, sometimes a few days more or a few days less, sometimes skipping a month or two. I assumed that it was a normal part of my period shutting down. What I didn't know was that a late menopause is another risk factor of uterine cancer, and the symptoms I had were suspicious.

I asked friends, some older than me, about their menopause experience. One woman told me that her mom was almost sixty when she stopped. Others said that their periods went crazy, like mine did, until they ended for good. A few said that they were regular right up until the end. Almost all told me how wonderful I would feel when I was finally post-menopausal and I didn't have to think about checking the calendar and having pads with me just in case. I also took a poll. All of the women I talked to had been younger than me when their periods stopped forever.

By the time my periods became erratic, the company I

worked for had moved out of state. I had lost my job and along with it my health insurance. The only health plan I could afford had a high premium and a very high deductible, so to avoid the out-of-pocket expenses I skipped my annual checkup. Not a wise decision.

Gradually, I began feeling out of sorts. I couldn't say exactly why I felt that way, but just that I was tired a lot and my body didn't feel quite right. I convinced myself that it was a normal part of menopause and aging. Next, I noticed subtle changes in what I thought was my diminishing period. The bleeding became much lighter. It turned to a watery blood-streaked discharge, and its timing was unpredictable. After a while, I had some sort of bleeding almost every day. I had none of the symptoms that usually accompanied my period, like mood swings and cramps, but I sometimes felt a little bloated around my middle, and I needed to urinate more often. Occasionally, I felt a mild pressure in my lower pelvic area. Except for the bleeding, all of the other symptoms were vague, barely noticeable. Yet, they concerned me enough that I researched them online.

I typed my symptoms into a search engine, and that led to a series of menopause forums and message boards. The word *cancer* showed up often. What I read there scared me. I dug deeper researching gynecological cancers on trusted websites like the American Cancer Society, the National Cancer Institute, the Mayo Clinic and other cancer hospitals. As I browsed through the warning signs for gynecological cancers, many of my symptoms matched.

I learned that not all women have the same set of symptoms for uterine cancer, but any abnormal bleeding or discharge, especially post-menopause, is cause for concern. Everything I read said to see your doctor if you have very heavy bleeding, bleeding that lasts longer than normal, bleeding that happens more often than every three weeks, or bleeding that occurs after sex or between periods. After I had done the research, the voice from the bluff, God's voice, whispered to me that I did have uterine cancer and I should make an appointment with my doctor right away.

"But, everything I've read says to be especially concerned if you're post- menopausal," I argued with Him. "And I'm not postmenopausal. I haven't gone a full year without a period."

Or had I? Maybe when my period started again after that eleven-month gap it hadn't been a period at all but instead the early signs of uterine cancer. The thought played over and over in my head as God continued to nudge me into action. Still, I hesitated to call the doctor's office and make an appointment. Finally, the bleeding became constant, and only then did I decide that I couldn't put it off any longer.

By then, Doctor P. had retired. I found another woman doctor, and I called her office to make an appointment.

"I've been spotting, but just a little," I told the receptionist on the other end of the line.

Denial made me portray the symptoms as less suspicious than they actually were. My Pap tests had always been normal. If I were at risk for a gynecological cancer, wouldn't something have shown up earlier, some little sign that something might be wrong? I tried to push thoughts of cancer out of my head. *Surely, God, you wouldn't allow me to have cancer!*

The soonest I could get an appointment was in two weeks. While I waited, I worried constantly. I spent hours online reading all about uterine cancer, and I learned that there are no routine tests or exams for early detection in women who are not at high risk and not having symptoms. A Pap test might find some forms of uterine (endometrial) cancers, but it isn't a good screening test.

I also discovered that the most common form of uterine cancer is called endometrial adenocarcinoma and like other cancers it is staged and graded. (I've only addressed endometrial adenocarcinoma in this book, but there are other more rare and aggressive kinds.)

Endometrial adenocarcinoma has four stages, the lower the stage the less invasive the cancer. In stage 1, the cancer is confined to the uterus. In stage 2, it has spread from the uterus to the connective tissue of the cervix. By stage 3, the cancer has moved further into the pelvic region and possibly the lymph nodes, and at stage 4, it has spread to other organs. Each stage is further broken into subcategories. For example, in stage 1A the tumor is confined to the endometrium (the lining of the uterus) or it has grown less than one half through the myometrium (also called the uterine "wall"). In stage 1B, it has grown more than halfway through the myometrium, but it has not spread beyond the body of the uterus. Uterine cancer comes in grades, too, 1 through 3. The higher the grade, the more aggressive and fast growing the cancer is.

The more I read about uterine cancer, the more frightened I became. I searched online for other non-cancerous conditions that fit my symptoms.

There was something called endometrial hyperplasia, a condition where the lining of the uterus is thicker than normal, usually because of too much estrogen. Endometrial hyperplasia isn't cancer, but in some cases it can lead to cancer of the uterus. One of the key symptoms of endometrial hyperplasia is abnormal bleeding. I read that in most cases it can be treated with the synthetic hormone progestin. I could deal with that diagnosis and treatment. *Dear God, please let it be hyperplasia.*

Or, I might have endometrial atrophy, a perimenopausal condition where the uterus lining thins out because a woman's estrogen levels are low. That could cause abnormal bleeding. *Dear God, please let it be endometrial atrophy.*

I also read that uterine or cervical polyps often cause spotting. That sounded even better. *Dear God, please let it be a polyp.*

I fumbled around the Internet searching for possibilities. Still, I kept going back to the message boards and forums where I read posts from women who had sets of symptoms similar to mine. Almost always, they had cancer.

Cancer stayed on my mind every night as I tried to fall asleep, and it was the first thing I thought about when I woke up in the morning. I imagined every scenario from finding out that it was nothing to planning my funeral. The night before my doctor's appointment I panicked. I called my friend, Karen.

"I know I have cancer!" I told her. I repeated some of the stories I'd read online. "Those women had symptoms just like mine, and all of them had cancer. They all had hysterectomies. Some of them are really sick and having chemo, and —

"You need to calm down," Karen interrupted. "Women with your symptoms who *didn't* have cancer aren't likely to be posting on those message boards. All you're reading there is bad news.

Stay positive! You don't know yet what's going on."

That sounded logical.

"And," she added. "I'm sure that there are thousands and thousands of women out there who have symptoms like yours and don't have cancer."

Well, maybe not thousands and thousands, but certainly not all women with my symptoms had uterine cancer. I'd read that most often bleeding and spotting between periods isn't cancer. That idea calmed me a little. But still, I had a nagging feeling that a cancer was growing inside me. No matter how hard I tried to chase it away, it stayed with me. Was Neville back, I wondered, or was it God trying to tell me something.

Later that night, I got on my knees and I begged, "Dear God, please hear my prayer. Please. Not cancer, not me!" Then I opened my bible to a random page and I saw these words: "Take up the shield of faith with which you can extinguish all the flaming arrows of the evil one." Ephesians 6:16. I felt then in my heart that what I had presumed was true. I had cancer.

CHAPTER 7
An Issue Of Blood

Dixie Carter died on April 10, 2010. Her character, Julia Sugarbaker, on the popular television show "Designing Women," had been caustic and sardonic, but in real life, Dixie Carter was a conservative Christian woman who wasn't afraid to share her faith. I remember one episode of "Designing Women" in which she sang a touching rendition of "How Great Thou Art." In an interview, Dixie said it was her mother's favorite hymn. It was my mother's favorite hymn, too.

A hymn wasn't all that Mom and Dixie had in common. Dixie Carter's obituary appeared in newspapers on Saturday, April 11, 2010. I remember the date because it was the eleventh anniversary of my mother's death, April 11, 1999. Mom had suffered from myelodysplastic syndrome, a form of pre-leukemia in which the bone marrow doesn't produce enough healthy blood cells. Her disease rapidly worsened into acute leukemia, and just three weeks after her diagnosis she went to be with the Lord.

Dixie Carter had cancer, too, uterine cancer, the aggressive kind. She died not long after her diagnosis from complications related to her disease. It was Dixie Carter's death from uterine cancer combined with the date of my mother's passing that finally provoked me to schedule an appointment with Doctor A.

I sat wrapped in a paper hospital gown waiting for the doctor to enter the examining room. The wait seemed like an eternity.

The night before, I'd scribbled on a piece of paper my family medical history and a list of my symptoms. When I arrived at the doctor's office, I handed the paper to the nurse. My written page ended with a note: *Doctor, I'm worried that I have cancer.* I hoped that my doctor was delayed because she was reading what I had written.

As I waited, I thumbed through the pages of a magazine without paying any attention to its pictures or its words. I sat silently praying that the doctor would be cheerful when she came into the room and assure me that I had nothing to worry about. When the door swung open, Doctor A. walked in holding my written list. She sat down on a little stool and rolled it close to me.

"So, Jean," she said in a thick Asian accent. "You are having some abnormal bleeding post-menopause. Correct?"

"I'm not sure I'm post-menopausal," I answered. I felt the muscles in my back tighten. "I went eleven months without a period and then it started up again."

She studied what I had written. "The discharge has just a little blood in it?"

"Yes." I felt the tension ascend into my shoulders. "But sometimes it's more like a light period. I think it's probably just menopause."

I wanted her to agree with me, but she said nothing as she continued to read through my list of symptoms.

"And it is irregular, the bleeding? Close together? Far apart?"

"Close together." I hesitated. "Lately, it's almost every day."

She stood up and set the paper on the counter. "Every day?" She sounded concerned.

"Sometimes," I replied ambiguously.

"And you have pressure in your pelvic region sometimes?"

She placed one hand on her lower pelvic area and patted there.

"Not often," I answered, "but yes, sometimes I feel a little heaviness there. It's probably just that I'm overweight."

Doctor A. asked me to lie down on the table. When she examined me, she spent a lot of time pushing and prodding around my belly.

"We need to get blood work," she announced. "I want to do that today and then a transvaginal ultrasound as soon as possible. Okay?"

As far as I was concerned, none of this was okay, but I had no choice. I had put my faith in God and promised Him that I'd move forward.

"Okay," I agreed. "Are you going to do a Pap smear?"

"Not yet," she answered. "I want to see first what the ultrasound shows."

"What about a C-125?" (The standard blood test for ovarian cancer.)

"Not yet."

While Doctor A. sat on the stool writing up a lengthy list of orders, we discussed my insurance policy. Then I decided to bring up the subject that we had both avoided.

"Do you think that I have cancer?"

A clumsy pause filled the room, a silence that needed no translation.

"Cancer is certainly a possibility," she said without looking at me. Then she stood up and patted my shoulder. "Do you have any questions?"

"No," I said.

I had a million questions, but I had already stuffed them into The Hidden Place. Doctor A. hadn't mentioned that I had many of the risk factors associated with uterine cancer. We both knew what they were. But none of that mattered now. The writer part of my brain kicked in with a quotation long buried in my subconscious: "Things without all remedy should be without regard: what's done, is done." Shakespeare. Lady Macbeth.

I was struck numb like Zechariah—speechless. What was done, was done.

A transvaginal ultrasound is a type of ultrasound performed with an internal probe. It sends sound waves that reflect off internal organs allowing the doctor to look closely at a woman's uterus, ovaries, cervix, and vagina. The following Monday morning, I got up early and prepared for the test. My instructions said to drink 32 ounces of water one hour before the scheduled exam. I had to down it all in 15 minutes. I'm never good with a full bladder, and I worried about it all the way through the half hour drive to the hospital. By the time I arrived, I was more than ready to go to the bathroom.

"We'll get you in for the exam right away," the receptionist promised.

Within a few minutes, I had changed into a hospital gown, a pretty cloth one this time, and I sat on an examining table in a small, softly lit room. Two brass lamps with cream-colored shades set on a pair of oak end tables. They cast a gentle glow on the peachy pastel walls giving the place a girly, home-like feeling. A television mounted high on one wall was tuned to "Good Morning America." On the show that morning, Robin Roberts interviewed tennis star Martina Navratilova about her recent breast cancer.

"I couldn't think. I couldn't move," said Martina about hearing her diagnosis. "I've been healthy all my life and all of a sudden I have cancer. Are you kidding me?"

Just then, the technician came into the room. She must have noticed that Martina's words on the television made me uneasy because she turned off the sound.

"You probably need to go to the bathroom," she chirped, way too perky for an early Monday morning.

Please, don't remind me!

She asked me to lie down on the table and then covered me, from the waist down, with a thin, paper sheet. I slid into the awkward position that women assume for pelvic exams.

"I always have painful PAPs," I warned her.

"I'll be gentle," she promised.

But as hard as she tried, and believe me she tried, she couldn't complete the exam. While most women have no problem at all enduring a transvaginal ultrasound, I was one of the unlucky ones. Finally, when she saw tears welling in my eyes, she gave up. She allowed me to run to the bathroom to empty my bladder. But I wasn't done with the exam yet. I needed an external pelvic ultrasound.

When I returned to the table, the technician pulled my gown up to expose my belly. Then she applied a cold gel. After that, she passed a small handheld instrument, called a transducer, back and forth across my skin. Sometimes, she lingered and pressed it firmly against certain areas of my pelvis.

"Any history of fibroids?" she asked.

"No," I said. "Why, do you see one?"

She smiled. "I'm not allowed to tell you. But I'm getting some good pictures."

Wonderful.

By the time she had finished, I was ready to be out of there. I dressed quickly and left the hospital. As I walked into the warm spring sunlight, I prayed, "God, please stay close to me." For the rest of that day, I tried not to think about the ultrasound results, but when I went to bed that night, I panicked. "God, help me!" Oh, how I wished that I would hear His voice just then and that I could see Him sitting at my bedside like my mother used to do when I was a sick child. Instead, God seemed so far away. What I did get from God that night was a snapshot. As I tried to fall asleep, He showed me a long-forgotten scene from my childhood:

When I was little, I was terribly afraid of wasps. Their buzzing reminded me of a fleet of World War II fighter planes flying overhead, and their dangling legs were eagles' talons, ready to grab me and carry me off to the place where monsters live. Okay, I'm exaggerating here, but to a little kid, wasps are scary. God's snapshot showed Little Me walking home from school on a hot September afternoon. When I got to my house, I saw a swarm of wasps buzzing around a bed of chrysanthemums near the back door. No way would I walk up that sidewalk and risk getting stung! So, I stood there and waited.

"What's the matter?" Grandma Lily called from her open upstairs window.

"Wasps!" I said.

"They won't hurt you."

"They will too!"

I might have been young, but I wasn't stupid. I knew that wasps sting and they especially like preying on little kids.

Grandma disappeared from the window and before long I saw her come out her back door wearing rubber boots. Grandma Lily always wore boots when she gardened, and not rain boots either. She preferred her old, clunky, black snow boots; the ones that came up above her ankles and had nappy, gray fur trim on their tops. She looked ridiculous dressed in her blue, flower-print housedress and those boots.

"Wait." she told me. "I'll be right back."

Grandma returned with the garden hose. She had the nozzle set to shoot a sharp stream of water, and she aimed it straight at the chrysanthemum plants. Pow! The spray hit the flowers hard causing wasps to explode in all directions.

"Run!" Grandma told me.

Was she kidding?

"Hurry up!" she commanded. "I'll hold 'em off. Run to the door."

I thought about obeying, but I stood firm. Then, in her best Methodist-church-choir voice, Grandma Lily sprayed the wasps and sang:

"*Onward, Christian soldiers,*
Marching as to war,
With the cross of Jesus Going on before . . ."

Bravely, Little Me slipped on the armor of God, and I raced triumphantly up the sidewalk and safely through the door. Thank you, Grandma Lily. And thank you God for the snapshot.

Thoughts of uterine cancer had been buzzing through my brain like angry wasps, and I needed to control them. I had to put on my armor and fight them head on. That night, as I slipped off to sleep thinking of Grandma Lily battling the wasps, I knew that if I had to fight cancer I could do it, and I'd do it with the determination of a Christian soldier. *Therefore, put on the full armor of God, so that when the day of evil comes, you may be able to stand your ground, and after you have done everything, to stand.* Ephesians 6:13. I was ready for the fight.

The next morning, Doctor A.'s nurse called.

"We're still waiting for some of your blood work," she said. "But, what we've gotten back so far looks good."

Thank you, God.

"However."

Oh-oh. Here it comes.

"The ultrasound showed that your uterus lining is a little thick, and Doctor is referring you to a gynecological specialist. We'll make that appointment today and get you in as soon as possible."

Robotically, I scribbled the new doctor's name and number on a yellow sticky note. The nurse put me on hold and returned a few minutes later.

"Jean, we've got your appointment set up with Doctor Z. on May 18th at 10 o'clock."

Almost three weeks away.

When I hung up the phone, I thought of something Corrie ten Boom once said. Remember her? She was the famous Dutch holocaust survivor and evangelist who wrote *The Hiding Place*. Corrie endured unspeakable cruelty and suffering in the Ravensbruck concentration camp in northern Germany, but she never lost her faith in God. Instead, Corrie ten Boom grew strong in adversity. "Let God's promises shine on your problems," she said. "When a train goes through a tunnel and it gets dark, you don't throw away the ticket and jump off. You sit still and trust the engineer." I love that quote. I remembered it often during those long three weeks.

My friend, Sarah, had given me an iPod Shuffle for Christmas and an iTunes gift card. I decided to load the iPod with Christian songs for support and healing. I downloaded Eric Nuzum's "Healing Waters," Daniel O'Donnell's "Be Not Afraid," and Steve Green's "In Brokenness You Shine." I listened to those and other healing songs every night before I went to bed. I meditated on their lyrics as I tried to fall asleep.

During those weeks, I thought of another quotation, this one by D.L. Moody: "Tarry at a promise, and God will meet you there." That quote led me to dig through the bible looking for God's promises about health and healing.

"But I will restore you to health and heal your wounds," declares the LORD. Jeremiah 30:17

"But for you who revere my name, the sun of righteousness will rise with healing in its rays." Malachi 4:2

"Is anyone among you sick? Let him call for the elders of the church, and let them pray over him, anointing him with oil in the name of the Lord. And the prayer of faith will save the sick, and the Lord will raise him up. And if he has committed sins, he will be forgiven." James 5:14-15 (ESV)

I started putting a smudge of olive oil on my forehead every night before I got down on my knees to pray. Then I said, "God, there are no church elders here to anoint my head with oil, but I call on you in the name of the Lord. Please hear my prayer of faith and heal me from cancer," and I added, "If that's what I have."

Do you see that I was in the Bargaining stage of grief? It was as if I were saying, "God, if I pray faithfully and anoint my head with oil, will you take this from me? Lord, if I stand on your promises, will you heal me?"

I am not a patient person, and I expected an answer right away. I expected to hear God's voice in my heart just as I had on the bluff. I thought that I might feel in my spirit an overwhelming sense of health and peace. But I felt nothing. Like Corrie ten Boom did, I tried to trust by faith that God was with me and that He heard my prayers. As best I could, I kept on praying and hoping and believing in His love.

I turned to the bible searching for stories about God saving people from near death. In the Old Testament, I re-read the familiar accounts of Noah and the flood, Jonah and the big fish, and Job, who had lost almost everything. At his worst, Job sat in the dust dressed in sackcloth, his skin covered in painful boils, and still he clung to God and expected God's help. Then, in the New Testament I read about the miraculous healings Jesus had done: curing a nobleman's son in Cana; healing Peter's mother-in-law in Capernaum; restoring health to a leper in Galilee; making the paralyzed walk again; casting demons from the mentally ill. Finally, I came across a familiar passage of scripture in the Book of Mark. It tells about when Jesus is on His way to Jarius' house to heal his little girl who is desperately ill and dying.

Jesus and His disciples were in Gennesaret, on the northwest shore of the Sea of Galilee, almost to Jarius' place when:

"A large crowd followed and pressed around him. And a

woman was there who had been subject to bleeding for twelve years. She had suffered a great deal under the care of many doctors and had spent all she had; yet instead of getting better she grew worse. When she heard about Jesus, she came up behind him in the crowd and touched his cloak, because she thought, 'If I just touch his clothes, I will be healed.' Immediately her bleeding stopped and she felt in her body that she was freed from her suffering.

At once Jesus realized that power had gone out from him. He turned around in the crowd and asked, 'Who touched my clothes?'

'You see the people crowding against you,' his disciples answered, 'and yet you can ask, 'Who touched me?''

But Jesus kept looking around to see who had done it. Then the woman, knowing what had happened to her, came and fell at his feet and, trembling with fear, told him the whole truth. He said to her, 'Daughter, your faith has healed you. Go in peace and be freed from your suffering.' Mark 5:24-34.

Some translations say that this woman had "an issue of blood." None specifically describe her issue, but I imagine that she had a bleeding issue related to her uterus. We can't know for sure. Still, she believed that if she could touch Jesus, even just a small scrap of His clothing, then she would be healed. And it happened! This woman reached out and touched Jesus' cloak, and the power went out from Him. He healed her instantly! If Jesus could do that for her, then certainly He could do it for me.

I put all the other scriptures aside, and I meditated on just that one.

"Dear Jesus," I prayed. "I am that woman. Two-thousand years later, here I am chasing You through the crowd of other pray-ers hoping that somehow You might hear my cry and see me running after You. If only I can touch You then maybe You'll sense my fear and also my faith and instantly heal whatever it is that's going on inside of my body. *Jesus!* Stop. Turn around. Look at me. I'm The Woman With The Issue Of Blood."

CHAPTER 8
The Law Of The Blood

While I waited for the appointment with the specialist, I thought a lot about The Woman With The Issue Of Blood. I felt a kinship with her, and I imagined what her life might have been like thousands of years ago in bible times.

At the beginning of my story, I told you about the day I got my first period. I told my mother that I was bleeding, and she gave me the necessary supplies and sent me on life's way. Menstruation was nothing to be ashamed of in the twentieth century. A first period meant simply a rite of passage, an ordinary part of growing up. But things were radically different in Israel in the first century when The Woman With The Issue Of Blood was a girl.

Let's imagine what it might have been like.

As a young girl, The Woman With The Issue Of Blood hadn't prepared to get her period. She couldn't know when it might begin. But when it happened, it was impossible for her to keep it a secret. If women in the 18th century bled into their clothing, then we can assume that women in the first century did too, or maybe they used rags like in my grandmothers' time, or animal hides. The sun is hot in Israel, and the women who lived there wore lightweight, loose fitting garments that absorbed moisture. So, if her mother didn't already know by seeing blood on her daughter's cloak, then certainly the daughter took her mother aside and whispered: "Mother, I am impure and unclean."

Impure? Unclean? Why would she say that? Because women in biblical times were shunned when they had their periods. It goes back to the Book of Leviticus in the Old Testament.

God gave Moses laws and instructions for the people of Israel, and some of those laws had to do with menstruation. Here are seven of those laws from Leviticus 15:19-28. I've named them "The Law of the Blood."

1. When you get your period, you will be considered unclean for seven days.
2. If anyone touches you while you have your period, that person must take a bath.
3. Anything you rest or sit on while you are menstruating will be considered unclean.
4. If anyone touches anything you rest or sit on during your period, that person must wash their clothing and take a bath.
5. If you have sexual relations with your husband while you are menstruating, then he is considered unclean for seven days, and anything he sits on is also unclean.
6. Any bleeding outside of your normal monthly period makes you unclean until it stops (and rules 2 through 5 apply).
7. Seven days after you "get well," you will be considered clean.

When The Woman With The Issue Of Blood got her first period, she understood those laws. She accepted that for a few days each month she would be thought of as unclean and undesirable.

Just as all women do, The Woman With The Issue Of Blood probably settled into her monthly routine and didn't give it much thought. As she matured she noticed the handsome young men around her and presumed that her future included a husband and children. Certainly, she lived unaware that her body held a secret, a predisposition to a gynecological disorder that would show up later in her life.

The bible doesn't tell us whether The Woman With The Issue

Of Blood got married and had children, but let's imagine that she did.

Relying on historical accounts from Old Testament times, we can imagine that the woman's parents chose her husband, most likely a man who believed in God. And then came a betrothal. The future groom and the bride's father negotiated a covenant regarding the bride's worth. A father, back then, considered his daughter property to be sold to the bridegroom. After Dad and the bridegroom agreed on a price and the groom made his payment, the couple became husband and wife. "Husband and wife" had a very different meaning than in our modern times when a preacher says, "I now pronounce you husband and wife." In biblical times, being husband and wife only meant that the girl was set apart exclusively for the boy she would eventually marry. The couple sipped wine from the same cup to seal their covenant. Then the groom left and went back to his parents' house where he stayed for one year. No visits, letters or messages to or from his wife. During their year apart, the groom prepared a home for his bride, and the bride prepared for her married life. Finally, after twelve months the couple reunited and celebrated with an extravagant wedding and a weeklong reception before they settled in to live together.

If The Woman With The Issue Of Blood began her menstrual troubles before the wedding happened, then most likely she never married. She would be unclean and unworthy of her bridegroom. And it gets even more complicated.

The Hebrew word "niddah" is used to describe a woman when she is menstruating. It literally means "one who is excluded or expelled." To be niddah meant that you were unclean and unfit to approach God. Can you imagine being unacceptable for God and barred from fellowship with other believers? The Woman With The Issue Of Blood was niddah. To be cleansed of her disorder, she had to be free from bleeding for seven days. Then on the eighth day she had to take two doves to the high priest. He sacrificed one as a sin offering and the other as a burnt offering. That was how the woman made amends to God for the sin of her bleeding.

I am so grateful that I was born after Jesus sacrificed his life for my sins. Otherwise, when my uterine cancer caused intermittent bleeding I would have been waiting outside my church with a cage full of sacrificial doves and counting the days until I was "clean" again so I could worship inside with my friends.

Ironically, doves are another connection that I have with The Woman With The Issue Of Blood.

On the day that I lost my job, at the precise hour that I left my workplace, a tame, white dove landed in my mother's flower garden, probably someone's lost pet or a dove that had been released at a wedding or funeral. The gentle bird immediately trusted my mother and even sat in her hand. Mom believed that God had sent the dove as a sign that He had a new plan for my life. She named her dove Lucky because he was lucky to be rescued. A year later when my mother lie dying in a hospital bed, I promised her that I would take Lucky as my pet. That was more than a decade ago, and Lucky still lives contentedly in a cage in my kitchen. The name Mom gave him reminds me that I am lucky that the blood of Christ saved me from my sins.

As sinful as I am, my Heavenly Father welcomes me into His presence and forgives me. When I was unclean and impure, He didn't hesitate to draw near to me. The only law that bound me was this: that I accept Jesus Christ as my Lord and Savior. When I was niddah, I could touch people, sit and rest wherever I liked and never worry that my condition would make me unfit for God or make others unclean. And, of course, Lucky was at peace knowing that he wouldn't end up as a sin offering!

I suppose that The Woman With The Issue Of Blood lived a life similar to someone with an infectious disease. Leviticus holds a rule for that, too: "The person with such an infectious disease must wear torn clothes, let his hair be unkempt, cover the lower part of his face and cry out, 'Unclean! Unclean!' As long as he has the infection, he remains unclean. He must live alone; he must live outside the camp." Leviticus 13:45-46.

The Woman With The Issue Of Blood probably wasn't contagious, so she didn't walk around with torn clothing and unkempt hair or with the lower part of her face covered. She didn't have to shout aloud, "I'm unclean!" Still, everyone knew that she was unclean and impure. They had to know so they wouldn't risk touching her or sitting upon anything that she had touched. I imagine that when her condition became chronic, she had to live alone. After all, it's difficult to be with someone and avoid touching them, even accidentally, or touching anything they sit and rest upon.

If The Woman With The Issue Of Blood were married and had children, and maybe even grandchildren, when she bled chronically her husband and children might have abandoned her. Most likely, they told her to leave their camp. She may have left to live alone—unclean and impure, away from the comfortable security of home. Her family had little choice; it was the law.

If I had gotten uterine cancer back in Old Testament times, when I most needed the love and support of my family and friends, I probably would have been told to go away, to leave the camp. Worst of all, I would have been considered unfit to approach God. Can you imagine facing cancer or any serious illness alone? What a sad existence The Woman With The Issue Of Blood must have led while her bleeding kept her from enjoying a happy, healthy life. For twelve years she lived in lonely isolation, desperate, friendless, and unfit for God. So what did she do? Did she quietly accept her illness and wait to die, or did she stand up and fight?

She fought! Mark 5:26 tells us that The Woman With The Issue Of Blood went to doctors hoping to be cured, and she suffered a great deal under their care. And remember, when her condition or its treatments caused her pain, she had none of the painkillers we have today. It was a miserable road to travel; still she kept trying to find a healing treatment. Few options existed. I suppose that she suffered not only physically from the primitive tests and remedies, but also emotionally. For more than a decade, this woman faithfully trusted doctors to heal her condition. In fact, Mark 5:26 tells us that she spent all of her money on doctors' bills. As a result, she ended up with nothing.

The Woman With The Issue Of Blood was sick, isolated from the world, and poor. The medical treatments hadn't made a difference. Instead, her condition grew worse. But the woman had one thing going for her—hope. After twelve years of constant failures, The Woman With The Issue Of Blood still refused to give up hope. She didn't say, "I'd better not get my hopes up again, because I can't stand another disappointment." She didn't say, "There's no hope left for my healing." Instead, she looked for the next hopeful option.

She knew of a man named Jesus, an amazing teacher, prophet, and healer. He was very popular and followed by crowds wherever He went. She'd heard stories of Him healing lepers of their incurable disease and making the blind see and the crippled walk. The Woman With The Issue Of Blood believed that Jesus could heal her too. But what would it take? How could she get to this great man, the one they called Rabbi?

Jesus had not yet saved us when The Woman With The Issue Of Blood considered going to Him for healing. The Old Testament law still existed. If she joined the crowds that followed Jesus and anyone recognized her, they would shrink away from her, afraid of being made unclean. They might even try to hurt her.

Can you imagine the thoughts that went through her head? What if they warned Jesus that she was unclean? Then she'd never get anywhere near Him. She was outcast, forbidden to touch anyone or to be touched. Yet, The Woman With The Issue Of Blood believed that this man named Jesus held her only hope.

The law forbade a woman to speak to a man in public unless he was her husband, so she couldn't just walk up to the Rabbi and ask Him to heal her. If she just touched Him, she knew it would be enough. But if she touched Him, then *He* would be unclean. Certainly, she didn't want to make the Rabbi unclean, but to touch Him was the only way that she could be healed. What a dilemma she faced! Jesus was her only hope. Yet, how could she approach Him? *Maybe*, she thought, *if I just touch the hem of His cloak He won't know that I've touched Him and made Him unclean. If I'm very careful, then afterward I can melt into the crowd and slink away.* The Woman With The Issue Of Blood made a plan, and a risky one at that.

The bible tells us that a crowd surrounded Jesus on that day in Gennesaret. Everyone wanted to be near Him, and the people pushed and jostled Him. I imagine that The Woman With The Issue Of Blood planned to get there before Jesus arrived. Most likely, she hid until He and the crowd walked in front of her.

Maybe she wore a scarf over her face to keep from being recognized.

As the crowd focused its attention on the Rabbi, she pushed her way through, touching countless people in the process and, by law, making them unclean. When she finally came up behind Jesus, she did the unthinkable. She touched the hem of His cloak. Can you imagine the risk that she took when she touched Him making Him unclean? Imagine her shame when Jesus turned around and said to her, "Who touched me?" Fear must have filled her heart. She trembled. Only seconds before she had experienced such joy and healing when she touched Him, but now The Woman With The Issue Of Blood dropped to her knees, ashamed of what she had done.

She confessed it all to Him. She told Jesus the truth: "I am the one who touched you, and worse I am impure and unclean. I touched you because I am bleeding outside of my period. I have been bleeding and outcast for twelve years, and I am so alone. Rabbi, I believe, that you have healed me. I felt the healing go out from you and into my body. I touched you because you heal people with incurable diseases, and now I am healed." I wonder if when The Woman With The Issue Of Blood made her confession the crowd shrunk away from her in fear and anger. How many had she defiled by her touch?

But what did Jesus do? He lovingly called her "Daughter." He wasn't at all worried that she had touched Him and made Him unclean. "Your faith has healed you," He said to her. "Go in peace and be freed from your suffering."

Can you imagine? At last, after twelve long years of scary bleeding and doctors and treatments that didn't work, The Woman With The Issue Of Blood was well again, clean and pure, and able to reunite with her family and friends. How happy she must have been to return to the camp! How relieved she must have been to shed her loneliness.

Of course, most of the story exists only in my imagination, but that's how I think it might have happened with The Woman With The Issue Of Blood.

Having cancer is a lot like living outside of the camp. It can be a lonely and depressing place. Cancer changes us, and if we're not careful it becomes us. It separates us and makes us feel different from others. With Cancer, we feel like we worry alone, pray alone, hope alone, and cry alone. But living with Cancer doesn't have to be lonely.

The author Wendell Barry writes, "Healing is impossible in loneliness; it is the opposite of loneliness. Conviviality is healing. To be healed we must come with all the other creatures to the feast of Creation."

Today, Old Testament laws don't bind us anymore. Today, those of us who back in biblical times would be shunned for our infirmities are welcome in Christ's church. That is why it is so important that we allow others to share in and help with our cancer journey. It isn't necessary to touch Jesus Christ in a literal sense to experience His healing. Today, He heals our emotional and physical needs through the aid of other people.

Throughout my cancer journey The Woman With The Issue Of Blood's strength, determination, and faith encouraged me. How bold and confident she was! If she hadn't been, she might have lived a sad and disheartened life.

Sometimes though, Fear managed to creep in as I awaited my appointment with the specialist. Neville tried to trick me again into thinking that I was broken and unfixable. There were days when I allowed the "what ifs" and "if onlies" to inch into my thoughts. But The Woman With The Issue Of Blood was steadfast in my mind. She had refused to let trouble stop her, and so would I. As I meditated on her character, God reminded me of the snapshot that He had given me of myself racing up the sidewalk through the swarm of angry wasps, protected not only by the powerful spray from Grandma Lily's garden hose, but also by the full armor of God. Like The Woman With The Issue Of Blood, I was brave!

God used her to inspire me. With certainty, I believed that the path to my healing was through faith in Jesus Christ. I had no idea what the specialist would diagnose, but I knew that I could do all things through Christ who strengthens me. Philippians 4:13 (KJV). If the doctor told me that I had cancer, I could accept the diagnosis. Like The Woman With The Issue Of Blood, I could face my disease strong and determined not to give up. I could press on and fight. If God's plan for me included a journey down Cancer Road, then I wouldn't travel it alone because the Rabbi, Jesus Christ, the Great Healer, would be with me. I believed that He would heal me just as He had The Woman With The Issue Of Blood all those years ago. In fact, I felt certain of it. After all, the bible says: Jesus Christ is the same yesterday and today and forever. Hebrews 13:8.

CHAPTER 9
Yellow Butterflies

I sat on the examining table in another small room, this one decorated in dated pastel wallpaper. A Barbie-pink curtain created a modest, little dressing area in one corner, and my clothing lay on a gray folding chair behind the drawn curtain. Covered again from the waist down in a white paper sheet, I waited for Doctor Z.

A snapshot flashed into my head. It showed a day, years before, when I'd sat in a doctor's office with my mother waiting for her test results. Mom had been bleeding mysteriously, too, but she had an issue of blood far worse than mine. As we waited that day, her white cell count was almost non-existent and her body grew weak from internal loss of blood. My heart had pounded then as I sat with my mom, and it pounded now as I awaited my own diagnosis. I wished that she were with me.

The first thing I noticed when Doctor Z. entered the room were his glasses, round, Harry Potter style, but smaller. He shook my hand, smiled at me, and sat down on the little rolling stool that all doctors seem to have in their examining rooms. He rolled close to me and asked the standard litany of questions.

"How long have you had symptoms? Do you have any pain? Are you taking hormone replacement therapy? Have your periods stopped altogether?"

While I answered him, I focused on the garish green bowtie that encircled his neck, Kelly green with a pattern of bright yellow butterflies. The tie's knot bounced up and down when he spoke making the butterflies seem to flutter. How strange, I thought. Not that he wore such a bizarre tie, but because yellow butterflies had been an important symbol for me, one representing God's faithfulness.

My first butterfly encounter took place a few months after I'd dumped Neville for Jesus. Back then, I enjoyed taking walks during my lunch breaks. Those walks were my alone time with Jesus, just the two of us trying to work out the details of my messed up life.

The publishing company where I worked then was adjacent to the motherhouse and retreat center for a group of Dominican nuns. The sprawling grounds rested on the same bluff overlooking Lake Michigan where I had met the Lord. The nuns allowed people to walk there as long as visitors followed the rules and remained quiet and respectful. A concrete path wound through a densely wooded area and ended in a natural prairie, and there among a sea of pink cosmos and wild lavender, the nuns had carved a large, rectangular vegetable garden. A gated white picket fence surrounded it, and inside the fence, hanging from a tall wooden pole, a scarecrow wore an old, tattered nun's habit. It looked almost spooky as the black cloak flapped wildly in the breeze. Except for that scarecrow, the woodland and prairie overflowed with the peace of Christ. For me, this was church. The only thing missing was heavenly music. My creative side wished for speakers in the trees softly piping the strains of old hymns.

When some people accept the Lord, their lives change instantly, but my Christian journey didn't begin that way. It emerged slowly while God led me through baby steps and taught me to listen patiently with all of my senses.

When I'd first heard God's voice on the bluff, I thought it would be easy to know His will. I believed that I could ask Him what I should do and that He would instantly tell me. Instead, I discovered that God is often silent.

In the weeks and months following my bluff-top conversion, I cried out endlessly to Him for help, but He didn't answer. Still, I vowed that I would not give up hope. Having heard His voice just once was enough for me to believe that He really did exist. After all, I couldn't have made up the words that I heard on the bluff that day when God spoke them into my heart. Surely it wasn't coincidence that the sun shone that morning, just as He said it would. These things alone were sufficient to keep me believing. My mistake, though, was that I thought if I prayed long enough and hard enough, I would find the golden secret to hearing God's voice whenever I wanted to.

I searched for Him. I looked in Christian books, especially those about the power of prayer, and I read my bible daily. I soaked up everything that Jesus taught about prayer, and I did everything I could think of to please Him. Yet, God remained silent.

Then, one summer day when I walked through the grounds of the retreat center, I decided to sit down in the grass and look out at the water just as I had the first time I'd heard Him speak. I waited for something miraculous to happen, and, of course, being the impatient person that I am, I expected it to happen right away.

I waited two minutes, maybe three, and then, frustrated, I thought, Okay, God. If you're not going to talk to me then maybe Neville was right—maybe you don't exist. That thought had barely formed when a small, yellow butterfly landed on my knee.

I whisked it away, got up, and went on walking. The butterfly flew alongside me. At first I didn't think much about it. But then I noticed if I changed direction, so did the butterfly. If I walked faster, it kept up with me. Then the most incredible thing happened. Several more yellow butterflies joined the first. I had no idea where they came from. They were just there. They fluttered around and seemed interested only in me. When they had my attention, or maybe I should say when God had my attention. He whispered five simple words into my heart: "I am with you always." Matthew 28:20.

For the rest of that summer, yellow butterflies became a symbol of God's faithfulness. I saw them everywhere: on stationery, greeting cards, posters, and in newspaper ads. They flew in front of my car, and they fluttered outside my office window.

One day, while I was cleaning my apartment, I felt God nudging my spirit. The building where I lived was going condo, and I had the choice of buying my unit or finding another home. God seemed to be saying, "Go." I called a realtor, and I set up appointments to look at houses, and during the next few weeks I looked at more than a dozen. Nothing the realtor showed me felt right—too big, too small, too expensive, too far away. Finally, one afternoon, she called me at work.

"I've found the perfect house for you."

I'd heard that before. "Where?" I asked.

She recited the address, a place about a mile away from my apartment building in a neighborhood that I was familiar with. I knew that I couldn't afford a house there.

"Just drive by and take a look," the realtor suggested. "This one feels right, and the seller is motivated. It just might fit within your budget."

So after work that day, I drove through the tree-lined streets toward the address the realtor had given me.

I found the place and parked near the curb out front. The ranch-style house set in the middle of a long block of cream-colored brick homes with tidy yards and quaint little gardens. The house looked attractive and it appeared well cared for. The front yard had several mature trees and shrubs that appealed to my gardening muse, and I noticed two window boxes that could use my attention. *I can't afford this*, I thought. And then I saw it, a yellow butterfly, wings outstretched, in the center of a large stained-glass sun catcher in the front window.

"Okay, God," I whispered. "This must be the place. Tell me. What should I do now?"

The realtor arranged a tour. The inside of the house wasn't much bigger than my two-bedroom apartment, but the floor plan made it look spacious. It had a large living room perfect for entertaining and an extra bedroom that I could use as an office. The back yard was a blank canvas awaiting the flower gardens that I had always imagined, and there was a garage. I wouldn't have to dig my car out of the snow anymore during harsh Wisconsin winters. Before we left, I got a closer look at the butterfly on the sun catcher. She looked ready to embrace me.

The house was more than I could afford, but still I made an offer. The seller rejected it. I placed a second offer, but the seller rejected that one, too. Discouragement set in. Neville loved that. He whispered to me, "Give it up." And after a little more coaxing, he convinced me that I was crazy to think that God sent me the butterfly as a symbol of His approval. "Call the realtor, and tell her to forget it," he said. So I did.

As I walked to the phone to make the call, I held the morning newspaper and glanced at the front page. A headline caught my eye: WISCONSIN STATE GOVERNMENT ISSUES LOW-INTEREST FINANCING FOR FIRST-TIME HOMEBUYERS. Instead of telling the realtor to stop working on the sale, I called to ask what she knew about this low-interest financing.

"I only just heard about it this morning," she said. "Let me find out more, and I'll call you back." After about an hour, the phone rang. "Great news!" she said. "You qualify for the financing. You can afford to offer the seller an amount closer to what he wants. Are you interested?"

"Of course I am!" I said. "How soon can you write up the offer?" I grabbed a scrap of paper and a pen so I could scribble down the details.

"I've already written it," she said. "How soon can you get here?"

"Right away," I replied.

I doodled a picture of the house on that scrap of paper, and I wrote the words THANK YOU, GOD near its front door.

That evening, the seller accepted my offer, and twenty-five years later I am still living in the house that God chose for me. My yellow butterfly sightings have decreased through the years, but sometimes God still sends me one in an unlikely time or place—like on my doctor's gaudy bowtie—as a gentle reminder that He loves me

Doctor Z. did a thorough exam. Then he told me to get dressed. "I'll be back in a few minutes," he promised, "And we'll talk."

The muscles in my neck stiffened. I felt cold as I slipped back into my clothing and sat on the examining table waiting and bracing myself for the worst.

"There's good news and not so good news," the doctor said as he closed the door behind him. "The good news is that nothing looks terribly suspicious on your ultrasound films." He leaned against the sink near the examining table. "You have some mild hyperplasia, but I don't see anything too worrisome there."

"And the not so good news?" I wondered.

He sat down on the stool and leaned slightly toward me. "The not so good news is that you have what I think is a large cervical polyp. It's positioned in a way that it didn't show up clearly on the ultrasound, and you're going to need a D&C to get rid of it."

A polyp! That's all? I let out a huge sigh of relief as tears welled in my eyes.

"So, it's not cancer?" I needed reassurance.

Doctor Z. rested his hands on his knees and sat up straight. "I'm pretty sure that the polyp is causing your bleeding. Of course, there can always be surprises, but I'm reasonably sure that everything is okay. We'll know more after the D&C."

I could have hugged him.

"I don't usually get emotional," I confessed, brushing away a tear trickling down my cheek, "but, Doctor, you've made my day . . . and, by the way, I love your bowtie!"

Before I left his office, I set up an appointment for the D&C to be done at the hospital the following week. Then I walked out the door into the bright sunshine silently thanking God for the good news.

Fifty-eight years old, and I had always been blessed with good health. I had never had a serious illness, and I had no good reason now to think that I was sick. The doctor's optimism convinced me that God was answering my prayers. When the D&C was finished I'd be healed of my bleeding. The yellow butterflies on the doctor's bowtie were God's sign, God's way of confirming it.

Or so I thought.

My longest experiences with hospitals had been when Grandma Dorothy and Mom were sick. In the back of my mind, I always carry those unpleasant memories with me. When I got into my car after leaving the doctor's office, a fleeting moment of dread swept through me. My mind flashed snapshots of Grandma and Mom's last days on Earth. I pushed those thoughts away, determined not to think of a hospital as just a place where people died. I didn't have good feelings about hospitals. I'd never been hospitalized, and the people I'd visited there were mostly old and dying. There were a few times when I'd seen friends in a hospital after they'd had babies, but other than that I'd known little of hospitals that wasn't related to death. For the next week, I fought to keep those scary hospital thoughts from entering my head.

I stayed busy, and I focused my thoughts on praising God for healing me. I hadn't received instant healing, like The Woman With the Issue of Blood, but a D&C to remove a troublesome polyp was an acceptable compromise, and the hospital stay would only be a few hours. I wasn't going to argue with God about the way He did things. In my Christian walk, I had learned that indeed He works in mysterious ways, and we should always expect the unexpected.

When I woke up on the morning of surgery, I was grateful that Sarah had offered to go to the hospital with me. Robert C. Byrd, the longest serving person in the U.S. Senate, once said, "One's family is the most important thing in life. I look at it this way: One of these days I'll be over in a hospital somewhere with four walls around me. And the only people who'll be with me will be my family." My immediate family was gone, but I could always rely on Sarah to be there. She was my family. Sarah arrived before dawn and we drove to the hospital. "It'll be fine," she said simply, and we didn't discuss the surgery the rest of the way there.

At the hospital, I put on a hospital gown and robe, and I slipped my feet into the terry cloth socks the nurse gave me, robin's egg blue with white, rubber treads on their bottoms. Sarah sat next to my bed in pre-op and waited with me. We made small talk while the nurse poked the back of my right hand with a long needle and inserted an IV.

"I've never had a general anesthetic," I warned her, wincing a little at the poke. "I don't know if I'm allergic or not." I watched a clear liquid begin to drip through the transparent IV tube.

"This isn't the anesthetic," the nurse said. "Just fluids to keep you hydrated. You've never had surgery?" She wrapped a blood pressure cuff around my arm.

"No," I said with a hint of pride. "I've never been sick enough to be in a hospital."

She squeezed the bulb on the blood pressure monitor, tightening the cuff till it hurt. "Well then, you've started with an easy one. It'll all be over in no time."

Sarah agreed.

A few minutes later, someone opened the curtain that separated my pre-op cubby from the others, and a handsome young man peeked in.

"Good morning," he said with a smile. "I'm Doctor K., and I'll be your anesthesiologist today." He sounded like a waiter in a restaurant about to take my order. "Any questions?" he asked.

"I've never been under a general anesthetic," I repeated, "and I'm a little worried about waking up nauseous and waking up at all."

"Don't worry," he said reaching down and wiggling my big toe through the terry cloth slipper. "We'll take good care of you. The nurse will put something into your IV, and by the time they wheel you to the operating room, you won't remember a thing. You'll be just fine."

"Okay," I said trying to force a smile. "I'll see you then, in a few minutes." What a dumb thing to say. I hoped that I'd be asleep before I entered the operating room to see the doctor and his "putting me under" apparatus.

Just as Doctor K. had promised, the nurse injected something into my IV, and then Sarah asked me to hand over my glasses.

"I'll hang onto these and see you in recovery, " she said. Then she gave my hand a little squeeze. "Don't worry. It'll be fine."

I heard the nurse say, "Think happy thoughts." Or maybe it was Sarah. The last thing I remember is my bed being wheeled through the operating room doors. I drifted off to sleep imagining that I were walking through the woods surrounded by yellow butterflies.

CHAPTER 10
One Bad Spot

I hope that you've never had a D&C. Not that it's a miserable procedure, it's not, but because it's usually done to investigate abnormal uterine bleeding or after a miscarriage. I hope that you haven't traveled either road.

If you've never had a D&C, then let me explain what it is. D&C is shorthand for "dialatation and curettage." *Dialatation* is a medical term that comes from Latin and means, "to enlarge or expand." When performing a D&C, the first thing the surgeon does is dilate, or open, the woman's cervix by using a medication to soften it. Once the cervix is dilated, the doctor uses a long, spoon-shaped instrument called a curet to scrape and remove the uterine lining. If a D&C is done to diagnose a problem, then a sample of the uterine tissue is sent to a laboratory for evaluation. The procedure takes less than half an hour under general anesthesia, and then, after an hour or two of recovery, you can go home. The doctor will probably suggest that you take it easy for a day or two and you might have some minor bleeding and cramping like you get with a period.

When I woke up in the recovery room, I had no pain. My body felt normal, like waking up from a solid night's sleep. A nurse sat next to my bed and offered me ice chips, and through the veiled anesthetic fog I realized that the D&C was over.

"Am I alright?" I asked. My words seemed to escape slowly and hang in the air.

"You're fine," the nurse answered wiping my lips with a damp washcloth.

"Cancer?" I said.

I hadn't planned to ask. What an odd sensation it was to have speech precede my thinking, but that's how my brain worked just after surgery.

"Doctor Z. will talk with you soon."

The nurse shoved another ice chip at me with a blue, plastic spoon, and my mind didn't fully process that she hadn't answered my question. Usually, worry would have set in then, but I was blissfully unaware as I lie there in my recovery bed waiting for whatever—.

I stared up at the ceiling at the endless rows of mottled, off-white tiles thinking about something that the American author Bertha Damon wrote: Hospital rooms seem to have vastly more ceiling than any rooms people live in.

A ghostly, ice blue figure suddenly appeared next to my bed. Through the fog I perceived someone dressed in surgical blues. I wasn't certain who it was until I saw the Harry Potter glasses.

"Cancer?" I asked thickly.

"Everything looked good!" said Doctor Z.

The tips of a red bowtie wiggled at the top of his shirt when he spoke. After that, I understood nothing he said. He probably explained the surgery, but what I heard was someone speaking like a grownup in a Peanuts cartoon, "Wah-wah-wha . . . wha-wha-wha-wha." Then, as quickly as Doctor Z. had shown up, he left me and went to care for his other patients. Had he really been there? Maybe I imagined him. Still not fully aware of what was going on, I felt my body in my wheeled bed being pushed beyond a double set of doors, down a series of long hallways and into an elevator. After what felt like Mr. Toad's Wild Ride, I woke up in a bed in a small semi-private room with Sarah by my side.

"How do you feel?" she asked.

I began to see clearly again, and I understood her words. "I'm okay," I responded. "A little groggy." I took the cup that Sarah offered me and sipped some orange juice through a straw. "Can we go home now?"

"Not yet," she said. "Drink more juice. They'll want you to use the bathroom before you leave."

I drank quickly, wanting nothing more than to leave the hospital and the D&C behind me. I prayed silently, thanking God that the journey was over. God had healed my issue of blood; the polyp was gone, the source of the bleeding was removed. Praise God, I was healed. PRAISE GOD!

I wonder if at any time prior to meeting Jesus, The Woman With The Issue Of Blood thought that she was healed. Did any of the ancient treatments work, but only for a while? I'm sure the doctors in her time didn't do D&Cs, but maybe a potion was enough to provide the illusion of good health. I can imagine her euphoria and the relief when her bleeding stopped. Just as easy, I can imagine the disappointment and fear when she noticed that it was back—that one red spot.

A few days after my surgery, the bleeding stopped altogether, and for the first time in months I felt normal. Doctor. S. had scheduled a follow-up for a week after the D&C, and I looked forward to it and getting a clean bill of health. I even felt smug about it, self-satisfied. I had escaped Cancer's trap. I had dodged the bullet, as they say. But then, two days before my appointment, the phone rang.

"Hi, Jean. This is Pam at Doctor Z's office. Doctor is wondering if you can come in sooner than Thursday?"

I hesitated before asking, "Why? Is there a problem?"

"We'd just like to reschedule you a little sooner," Pam said. Her voice sounded a little too chipper, and she hadn't answered my question. "How about tomorrow morning, or even sometime this afternoon?"

This afternoon! Any sense of peace that I had left me then, and Neville whispered—no, he shouted—

"See, Jean. I told you so. You're sick…You have cancer…. cancer…. cancer!"

I thought I heard him laugh.

I rescheduled the appointment for the next morning, and then I panicked. I called Sarah and also my friend Karen, and I told them about my conversation with Pam. Then I decided that I couldn't wait until the next day. I called the doctor's office.

"I'm really concerned," I said to Pam. "If there's something wrong with me, I'd rather not wait until tomorrow to find out. Can I still come in today?"

She put me on hold, and when she came back she said, "Can you be here in an hour?"

My heart raced.

Several minutes later, Karen and I were in her car making the half hour drive to the doctor's office. We arrived a few minutes before one, and the waiting room was empty. I felt relieved about that. It meant that I wouldn't have to sit worrying in a room filled with women, most of them young, healthy, and pregnant.

Pam ushered Karen and me into one of the examining rooms and promised that Doctor Z. would be with us soon. I sat on the examining table, shivering slightly from anticipation, and Karen sat calmly on the folding chair near the curtained changing-room area. We were barely settled when Doctor Z. came in holding a file folder. He shut the door, and I introduced him to my friend.

"Well," he said. "I got the results of your D&C this morning, and we have a little problem. The hyperplasia— remember, that thickened area of your uterus—has some cells that are premalignant."

I grabbed onto that word *premalignant*. It didn't mean cancer.

"And," the doctor continued, "There's one little bad spot."

Karen and I exchanged a quick glance wondering which one of us would ask the obvious question.

"By little bad spot do you mean cancer?" I said.

"Oh, sure," he answered, smiling, trying to put me at ease.

Oh— sure!

"I have cancer." I said it matter-of-factly, letting the words sink in. Then I went completely numb. I experienced one of those headstone moments that I told you about earlier. I withdrew into a place so deep inside me that neither Cancer nor Fear could find me. The questions I asked then sounded mechanical and almost rehearsed.

"What happens next?"

"You'll need a hysterectomy," Doctor Z. said.

"And the prognosis?"

My brain functioned as if it were separate from [...] soul. My mouth went dry, my heart pounded, [...] noticed.

"The prognosis is good!" he assured me. "The kin[d...] you have is called adenocarcinoma. That's a cancer tha[t...] the glandular lining of your uterus. Ninety-five percent [of...] cancers are adenocarcinomas. There are worse kinds o[f...] cancer, but you have the good kind."

I guess that was positive news. If I had to have canc[er...] good kind was . . . well . . . good. I looked at Karen, an[d...] managed a reassuring smile.

"Pathologists grade cancers," Doctor Z. explained. "You[rs is...] Grade 1, which means it's well differentiated."

"Well differentiated?"

"That means a low grade, less aggressive cancer, one that [is...] more responsive to treatment," he continued. "Most of the time[s] we catch these cancers early, and a hysterectomy is the only treatment you'll need. Once it's out, it's over."

I sucked in a long breath and let it out slowly as the weight of the past several minutes settled down on me and pushed me deeper into The Hidden Place.

"Can you do it laparoscopically?" I asked.

Karen looked at me as if to say, "Are you planning to wear a bikini any time soon?" We shared an addiction to food and the predisposition to plumpness. I didn't like the idea of my belly being sliced wide open.

"Absolutely," Doctor Z. answered.

"How soon?"

"Next Monday."

That was less than a week away.

When I researched the possibility of cancer, even before I had the initial exam with Doctor A., I had read that it's important to have a family member or friend with you when you get the diagnosis. The reason is that they can think clearly while you cannot. I remembered this, and I asked Karen if there was anything that I had forgotten to ask the doctor. She couldn't think of anything, but she clearly repeated to Doctor Z., and to me, what she had heard him say and what she had understood it to mean. I

knew that once the numbness wore off
relentlessly, and Karen would be there to
Grandma Lily had been there to stand
[...]e. Karen would reassure me and remind
[...] said.
[...] meeting with an apology. "Based on
[...] ultrasound and when I did the D&C, I'm
[...]ointed at the pathology report clipped to
[...]der. "Especially after telling you that it
[...]er. I'm sorry, but we'll take care of it."
[...]alked out of his office without speaking. I think
[...] to dissolve into tears once we got outside, but
[...] style.
[...] taking this well," she said as she unlocked the car
[...] be all right, " I answered flatly, and I said to myself, *God*
[...]*an.*
[...] believed that, but I didn't like not knowing what His plan
[...]s. I'm not a spontaneous kind of gal. So when God says, 'Come, follow me," I find it hard to grab hold of His hand and go skipping merrily alongside Him. Instead, I extend my hand cautiously, and I cringe a little when He takes it. I want to absolutely know how I'm going to get from here to heaven, and I want to be certain about what heaven is like before I get there. I don't like surprises.

Linda—Remember her? My friend whose anger at God made her feel ugly?—Linda had told me about a trip she took to a beach in southern Florida. It was during the time when her mother was nearing the end of her life.

"I walked alone in the wet sand," she said, "and I turned around to see if there was one set of footprints or two. Guess what? There was only one."

Having seen only her own footprints, Linda gave up on God. She decided that she walked alone in her trouble. And because of that, Linda met the future feeling ugly and afraid, and it made facing her mother's cancer almost unbearable.

I needed to find God in my cancer if I were to face it with hope. I had to believe that He was there, and whatever He had planned, I had to let Him take my hand and walk me through the valley to wherever it was that we were going. I wouldn't look back searching for footprints. Instead, I planned to keep my eyes set straight ahead, believing as best as I could in the words of Isaiah 48:17: "This is what the Lord says— your Redeemer, the Holy One of Israel: 'I am the Lord your God, who teaches you what is best for you, who directs you in the way you should go.'"

Take my hand, oh Lord, and direct me through this cancer.

On the ride back with Karen, my thoughts overflowed with everything I needed to do before the surgery. I called Sarah from my cell phone and told her about my diagnosis. She promised to be with me at the hospital. Then, I made a mental to-do list. I wanted to get home, go online, and read everything I could about endometrial adenocarcinoma, well-differentiated, grade 1.

I thought of something I had read, just the night before, something a Christian friend posted on her Facebook status. It was a quotation she liked by Norman Vincent Peale: "When a problem comes along, study it until you are completely knowledgeable. Then find that weak spot, break the problem apart, and the rest will be easy." I figured the more I learned about my kind of cancer, the easier it would be for me to understand what cancer meant for my future and also what I had to do to fight it. Neville would try everything in his power to break me down. Fear was my weak spot. I had to strengthen myself for the battle.

As a perceptive reader, you might already see that I had set myself up to fall into Neville's trap. My thoughts immediately turned to what *I* could do to break the problem apart, what *I* could do to strengthen my weak spot, what *I* could do to fight Neville. My plan didn't include help from the Body of Christ, His people.

Sometimes, God allows us to bring down an evil giant all by ourselves, like David did with Goliath, but most often He expects us to join with other believers in the fight. As the saying goes, there is strength in numbers.

Remember Joshua and the Battle of Jericho? God made Joshua the commander of His army. He told Joshua to march around the city "with all the armed men." And to that army, God added seven priests blowing trumpets. It took Joshua working together with the army and the priests to make enough noise to bring down the city wall. Joshua's single, small voice wasn't enough to fulfill God's plan.

I hadn't learned how much I needed the Body of Believers, nor could I anticipate the role they would play in my fight. But I was about to find out. I extended my arm and offered God my right hand. And yes, I cringed when He took it. Together, we began my journey into cancer.

CHAPTER 11
Frozen Tears

In the classic film "Meet Me in St. Louis," little Tootie Smith, dressed in her nightgown, rushes down the staircase in a fit of anger. Her anger explodes into tears as she fights the idea of her family moving from their comfortable home in St. Louis to a place in New York City. She runs through the foyer and out into the cold winter night, and there, in the snow, Tootie ambushes the family of snowpeople she'd built in her front yard. She grabs a makeshift wooden musket from the hands of a soldier snowman and, again and again, she slams it into him and the rest of her snowpeople whacking off their heads making snow fly in all directions. "Nobody's going to have them!" she sobs. "I'd rather kill them if we can't take them with us."

Instead of smashing God's windows, Tootie smashed her snowpeople to death.

Grandma Lily might have had some advice for Tootie: "Don't cry too long in the winter, or your tears will freeze." Grandma enjoyed quoting proverbs, and she particularly liked that one.

The proverb conjured in me an image of Tootie Smith crying over her dead snowpeople with icicles hanging from her chin. Of course, what Grandma said wasn't literal. It was only wise advice about life's seasons. We called Grandma's proverbs "Lilyisms". The key words to notice in her Tears in Winter proverb are *too long*. Grandma might explain it this way.

"When winter hits you like a nor'-easter, don't wallow in self-pity too long. There's a season for crying, but seasons change. Get past your tears. Face life head on! If you don't, you'll end up old and bitter."

I learned from Grandma Lily not to cry.

Grandma's life had been tough, and by the time I was born she was well beyond tears. My grandfather had died suddenly at age thirty-six, leaving Grandma alone, a young widow raising my dad, an only child, who was just nine years old. There was little money, and Grandma took a job as a matron at The Orthopedic School, a school for children suffering from polio and other muscular disorders. She did what certified nursing assistants do today only without modern technology and helpful equipment. Somehow, Grandma found enough physical strength in her five-foot-five, one-hundred-twenty pound body to lift dozens of children, from feather-weight babies to gangly teenagers, and she lifted them multiple times each day. She lifted them in and out of their beds, wheelchairs, whirlpool baths, and iron lungs. She held their hands, dried their tears, and told them stories. And when she came home at night, tired and hurting, she never complained.

Grandma worked that job for more than thirty years, and when she retired the school had a big party for her. The children cried when it came time to say goodbye, and so did some of the teachers. But Grandma scolded them.

"Don't you cry," she said. "Do you want your face to freeze like that?"

She made an ugly face, and the children laughed.

When I wander through life's valleys seeking a way out, my problem isn't that I cry too long, but that I don't cry at all. When my mother died, I didn't cry. I didn't cry during my dad's nine-year battle with Alzheimer's disease, or when a family member died of alcoholism; not even when a friend committed suicide, and especially not when I learned that I had cancer. I skipped the season of tears, and I went straight to facing life head on. And, as several of my friends pointed out—that's not normal.

Do you know the inky kind of darkness where you can't see beyond your nose? I'd experienced that sort of darkness on a balmy summer night when I vacationed in Ephraim, Wisconsin. The new moon had its dark side toward Earth, and when I stepped outside the small cabin on the bay I saw nothing. The world had disappeared, and there I stood alone with my God. My eyes seemed sightless, like those of Bartimaeus, the blind beggar sitting alongside the road on the way to Jericho. Remember him? He shouted, "Jesus, Son of David, have mercy on me!" And the Lord heard him, and He came and healed him. As I faced my cancer, I felt a similar darkness inside of me. I wondered would God hear me? Would He be merciful? Would He come and heal my cancer?

Sometimes we need darkness to see God. We need to fall into that black hole where tears are frozen and nothing exists but numbness and Him.

The Woman With The Issue Of Blood, with boundless unshakeable strength, and totally alone, kept plodding forward always believing that someone could heal her. I've never imagined her crying, but only facing life head on. Confronting my cancer, I wanted to be like her, steadfast and strong. I imagined that she spent her hours of darkness in solitude, alone with her thoughts, praying to God—instead of crying. Maybe she was more like me than I ever imagined. Maybe the only way she could accept her circumstances was to go numb, to sink deep into that place where nothing evil can force out the tears.

I don't remember when my chronic numbness set in. I only remember tromping through my crises without bawling. In fact, I've boasted to friends that if there's ever an emergency, I'm the person you want around. I tune out the bad stuff. The situation becomes like a movie to me, or a plot in a book. Pure fiction. Is anyone among you sick? No problem, you don't have to call the elders of the church like James instructs in the bible (James 5:14). Just call me. I guarantee that I'll calmly dial 911, state the problem, and provide aid until help arrives. After that, I'll stuff the reality of what happened into The Hidden Place and move on. I refuse to feel pain because I'm afraid that it might be more than I can bear.

Numbness is an enemy of perception. It creates a façade that others perceive either as emotionally cold or emotionally strong. I've been called both. But in reality, I'm not entirely present. When

I enter one of life's valleys, I slip into what I call "robot mode," functioning without feeling. I bury my connection to human suffering way deep inside in that safe, tear-free place.

"You're a much better person than I am," my friend Linda said. We were in my living room engaged in a conversation where I tried to be supportive during her mother's illness. "When you went through everything with your folks, you didn't lose faith in God, and you never once cried." She pointed to a tear trickling down her cheek, and then she raised her left hand toward me as if to say, "Stop!" until she regained her composure.

I didn't see that she fought hard trying not to cry in my presence. To me, support meant getting Linda to find her faith again. This is a hazard of numbness combined with Christianity. It allows empathy when a person moves forward in adversity with faith, but it sometimes prohibits sympathy when someone is bitter and angry with God.

"You need to let God back into your heart," I said, ignoring Linda's tears. "He's the One who can help you through this."

"Oh really?" she answered. "Tell me. Where is my merciful God? I'm not asking Him for anything for myself. I'm asking Him to put Mom's cancer into remission and to stop her suffering. But He keeps telling me no. How is that merciful? How is He helping me through this? The truth is that God doesn't understand what I'm going through—or maybe He just doesn't care."

She looked away, refusing to make eye contact with me. I skipped right over Linda's pain, and I dove head first into the New Testament.

"But God *does* understand," I argued. "Jesus understands suffering. *He* cares! God allowed Jesus to suffer terrible things. But they had to happen. It was God's plan for us. If He didn't allow Jesus to suffer and die, then we wouldn't have the promise of eternal life."

I added some gibberish about bad things happening to good people since the beginning of time.

"Everyone has an end story," I concluded.

Don't cry too long in the winter, Linda, or your tears will freeze. Quit crying. Be strong.

My friend sat there stone-faced. She was a Christian, and she could recite John 3:16 just as well as I could.

"Think about that," she said, griping the armrests and pressing her body into the back of the chair. She looked at me. "God did that to His—own—son! How is it loving and merciful when a father stands back and watches while someone tortures and murders his child?"

Linda had rearranged her anger with God. Now she aimed it at me.

"You're not getting it," I told her.

My voice sounded like a Pharisee standing on a street corner, pious and spewing superior knowledge of the scriptures. but I didn't care.

"It's all about sacrifice," I said. "In the Old Testament, people sacrificed their best animals as a way to show God that they loved Him more. That's why God sacrificed His own son, Jesus, to show us that He loved us even more than His own flesh and blood. And remember, Jesus was God, so it was like God saying to us, 'I love you even more than I love myself'."

As truthful as that was, my words sounded stiff and meaningless. Linda didn't need a bible lesson. She needed a hug and someone to listen to her anger and welcome her tears, but I didn't see that. I had disconnected from her suffering and jumped right into applying bible first aid.

"Thanks for trying," Linda said. "But no thanks."

Clearly upset, she got up and prepared to leave. Linda and I have martyrdom in common. We like to muddle through our crises all by ourselves. We chant that familiar chorus, Thank you for offering, but no thanks.

"So, you're an atheist now?" I said.

"Let's just say I'm a non-believer," she said, shutting the door behind her.

Linda left feeling worse than when she had arrived, but I stuffed that reality into The Hidden Place. I shook my head and wondered why my friend didn't get it. It was so clear to me: Dry your tears and move on. Buck up and face those circumstances, and above all, face them with faith! Obviously, this is not always what someone needs to hear when they're walking through a valley, and I regret my conversation with Linda that day. Doubt and anger were normal emotions for someone in Linda's situation. God understood her feelings. Why couldn't I?

I faced my cancer diagnosis frozen. I didn't allow myself to need help, and I didn't allow myself to doubt God or to be angry with Him. Doubt and anger were normal emotions given that Doctor Z. had suggested that I didn't have cancer and then told me that I did. But I can honestly tell you that in my numbness I felt only Neville's occasional tugging and a tiny bit of relief. I had sensed all along that a cancer was growing inside me. I even suspected it following the D&C, but I brushed it off blaming Neville's taunting. I think now that what I sensed was God preparing me for the journey.

Like The Woman With The Issue Of Blood, I lived my life an isolated believer, and in a way, I, too, was cast from the camp.

I've told you that my family left their church not long after my confirmation. That began a pattern of my little family withdrawing. As my parents' worlds became smaller, so did mine. I learned to be afraid around people, and before long that led to chronic panic attacks that began in my twenties and continued. They got worse in adulthood as valleys piled one onto another: stress from the job loss, my parents' illnesses and deaths, and then financial worries.

I never made it all the way back to church because being there among the Body of Christ literally made me sick. I entered the sanctuary, sat in the back, and fought overwhelming feelings of fear and dread as a panic attacks ripped through me. Imagine being in a burning building with all the exits blocked. It felt like that. I was close to the exit, but I couldn't get out. When I stood in church to sing hymns and join in the prayers, my legs turned to jelly and I felt faint. No one around me noticed because outwardly I was friendly and I didn't appear ill. Sunday mornings were torturous as I got ready for church and fought the anticipatory anxiety. I wanted to be a part of the congregation and fellowship with other believers, but my disability robbed me of those activities. Instead, I rushed out into the fresh air after services and withdrew, literally and figuratively, to home and The Hidden Place.

Of course, that was no way to honor and worship God, and

I'm sure that Neville loved it. But the joy he found in my isolation was groundless. Sickness pushed me nearer to God. As much as I hate the isolation that came with my panic disorder, it brought me nearer to the Lord as I sought a way out. I think this was also true of The Woman With The Issue Of Blood. As she faced her illness, she grabbed hold of God's hand, hung on, and turned toward Jesus. She knew that in her isolation she couldn't make the journey alone.

In Exodus 17:8-13, there's a little story about a war between the Israelites and the Amalekites. It's only six verses long, but it holds a powerful lesson.

"The Amalekites came and attacked the Israelites at Rephidim. Moses said to Joshua, 'Choose some of our men and go out to fight the Amalekites. Tomorrow I will stand on top of the hill with the staff of God in my hands.' So Joshua fought the Amalekites as Moses had ordered, and Moses, Aaron and Hur went to the top of the hill. As long as Moses held up his hands, the Israelites were winning, but whenever he lowered his hands, the Amalekites were winning. When Moses' hands grew tired, they took a stone and put it under him and he sat on it. Aaron and Hur held his hands up—one on one side, one on the other—so that his hands remained steady till sunset. So Joshua overcame the Amalekite army with the sword."

Think about that. For a while, Moses held off the Amalekites all alone holding up his hands, but finally, he couldn't do it by himself anymore. I wonder, did he ask Aaron and Hur to help him, or did his friends see his trouble and rush in to hold up his hands? Moses seems like a pretty independent guy, so my feeling is that it was Aaron's or Hur's idea to grab onto his hands and hold them up. In either case, the story shows that we believers need help to win our battles.

If you look a bit farther into the bible, in Isaiah 41:10 you'll find that God says this: "Do not fear, for I am with you; do not anxiously look about you, for I am your God. I will strengthen you, surely I will help you, surely I will uphold you with My righteous right hand." (NASB) God holds us up. When we grow weary and feel like we're about to lose the battle, He brings in help to hold us up.

When I gave the eulogy at my mother's funeral, I told the story of Moses, Aaron, and Hur. I used it to illustrate the unexpected helpfulness of family, friends, and strangers during Mom's illness. When she was sick, God brought people to meet our family's needs, and He sent them precisely when we needed them.

Facing my cancer, I remembered that my mother's tears had been frozen, too. She hadn't cried when she got her diagnosis and when the doctor told her that she had just a few weeks to live, nor did she cry in her last days. Instead, she retreated into numbness and held tight to God's hand.

"We're all headed to the same place," she told me. "I'm just walking on the road a little ahead of you."

She asked me to bring two items to her hospital room, a small, framed photograph of her grandmother and a china sparrow that had belonged to her mother, Grandma Dorothy. I understood, later, that the photograph and the china sparrow were Mom's Aaron and Hur. When she felt like she couldn't fight the war alone, she relied on thoughts of her mother and grandmother in heaven holding up her hands. The sparrow also reminded her of a familiar scripture verse that I found underlined in her Bible, Luke 12:7. "But even the very hairs of your head are all numbered. Fear not therefore: ye are of more value than many sparrows." (KJV) Mom had underlined the words *fear not*.

In the hospital the night before she died, my mother sat up in bed, and she said her name. "Betty Fischer!" She had been too weak to speak, but now her voice rang strong and firm. It startled me.

"Why did you say your name?" I said.

She pointed to a corner of the room. "Because He asked me." She said it as if I should know.

"Who asked you?" I wondered.

She stared at the photograph of her grandmother on the nightstand next to her bed. The expression on her face made me believe that the two of them were engaged in a silent conversation about my inability to understand. Then she looked at me and pointed again across the room.

"He asked my name," she repeated. "The One in the long, white robe."

With frozen tears, from her safe, numb place, my mother had asked God for help, and He sent it. Isolation had kept her from the Body of Believers, but God understood. He sent people to help with her physical needs in the hospital, and He sent spiritual help from the One in the long, white robe. *And my God will meet all your needs according to the riches of his glory in Christ Jesus.* Philippians 4:19.

When Doctor Z. told me that I had cancer, things went quiet in my head. When I'm quiet in my head, I know that I'm afraid and escaping deep inside of me into my unreachable, tear-free place. I didn't want to face my hysterectomy with a numb spirit, and I didn't want to face it alone. God's presence was all around me, and I knew that he would provide for me. Still, I was too frozen to offer even a small prayer for my own healing.

"Don't cry too long in the winter, or your tears will freeze." Grandma Lily's words echoed in my heart. My tears had frozen as I lingered too long in the winter of thinking that I could handle the valleys all by myself. When I remembered Grandma's proverb, I thought of her again, singing "Onward Christian Soldiers" as she stood in the gap between the wasps and me.

God sometimes uses memories to push us forward. Remembering Grandma Lily and the wasps and hearing that song in my head reinforced the idea that I needed friends to stand in the gap between the cancer and me. I couldn't fight it alone and be successful. My spirit had frozen and my hands were tired. If I couldn't hold them up, then I risked losing my faith and also my battle with Cancer. But without a church home, whom could I call on to stand in the gap? Who would hold up my hands? I knelt and prayed, "God, please send me my Aaron and Hur."

CHAPTER 12
Cyber Jesus

Several years before my diagnosis, Karen and I sat in Wilson's Coffee and Tea sipping hot Black Forest mochas.

"These are so good!" I said. "I'm going to tweet about them when I get home."

A dribble of chocolate-cherry foam spilled over the rim of Karen's mug, and she reached for a napkin to wipe it. "You're going to do what?"

"I'm going to tweet about these on Twitter." I said it smugly. I knew she didn't have a clue what Twitter was, and I sort of liked it that I was technologically superior to my friend who could do little more than search the Internet with her purple iMac.

"I think you're more than tweeting," Karen responded. "I think you've flown over the cuckoo's nest. What's a Twitter?"

If we had that conversation today, there's no question that Karen would know about Twitter, LinkedIn, Facebook, and similar social media sites. More than 2 billion people use the Internet worldwide, and of those 500 million use Twitter.

I swirled the coffee in its cup and watched the last remnants of the barista's carefully designed foamy autumn leaf disappear. "Twitter is where you go to meet people in cyberspace," I said.

"Isn't this good enough?" Karen looked around at the crowded coffee shop and gestured.

"Good enough for what?" I said.

"To meet people!" she answered. "These are real people. You don't know who you're talking with when you're online. I'd stay away from those Internet places. They're creepy."

In a way, I agreed with Karen. There are a lot of evil things lurking in cyberspace, and you need to be careful what you communicate and with whom.

I joined Twitter and Facebook mostly because of my work. Both provide a way for me to connect with Christian writers all over the world. But when I choose online friends, I try to be discerning. I choose them based on a shared interest in books, writing, and Christ. I'm not one of those people who will "friend" you if you "friend" me. I want to know a little bit about you first. If The Woman With The Issue Of Blood had been able to go online, she might put it this way: "I want to know which tribe you belong to and who is your God."

In the years since that conversation with Karen, I've gathered almost two thousand Facebook friends and hundreds of followers on Twitter. Some I correspond with daily, but I've not met any of them face-to-face.

When I got home after Doctor Z. told me that I had cancer, the first thing I did was to jump onto my social media sites and post a quick note: *Bad news today. Diagnosed with uterine cancer.* I don't know what I thought I'd accomplish by doing that. I guess I just needed to tell someone. I'm an open book when it comes to most of my life's events, and I don't keep many secrets.

The next thing I did was to search again for information about my specific kind of cancer. I needed reassurance that I was going to be okay. What I really wanted was to be absolutely certain that the diagnosis of adenocarcinoma, well-differentiated, grade 1 wasn't a death sentence.

My search led to several secular online cancer support groups, and I signed up to participate in one of them, a forum designed specifically for women with uterine cancer. After I had signed up as a member, I clicked a tab on the web site marked Support. There I found recent posts with headings like: MY PATHOLOGY REPORT—NOT GOOD NEWS; HELP. I'M FALLING APART!; IT CAN HAPPEN TO ANYONE, IT HAPPENED TO ME; DEAR

GOD, NOW IT'S IN MY LUNGS! I read the horror stories connected with the headings, and panic shot through my body all the way to my fingertips as they flew across the keyboard. I typed my own plea: *Help! I was just diagnosed with uterine cancer, adenocarcinoma, well-differentiated, grade 1. I'm having a hysterectomy next week, and I'm scared. I need support and advice.*

Within an hour, I had several replies:

"Don't trust your gynecologist. You need someone who specializes in gynecological oncology. Read the boards on this site, and you'll find women who needed a second surgery after their gynecologist botched the first one. Watch out."

"Don't go to your local hospital. Find a cancer hospital, and even if it costs more than your insurance will cover, go there. We're talking about your life."

"I'm sorry to hear about your diagnosis. I was diagnosed six months ago. I'm scared, too, because my mom died of uterine cancer. She died three months after her diagnosis."

I closed out of that forum. I shut down my computer and sat frozen staring into space. Neville loved it.

"See, Doctor Z. lied to you," he whispered. "I think he's hiding something from you. He reassured you that you'll be okay, but you're sicker than he let on, and you're going to die. You're like the women on that forum, facing your mortality, sinking deeper into the pit—"

And closer to you! That thought came from heaven. Somewhere up there, Moses held up his hands, and I came out of my daze ready to fight. I got it! The farther I let myself sink into a pit of despair, the closer I got to Neville.

I turned the computer on again. This time, I searched for the list of scriptures that I'd made and meditated on before my D&C. I found them, and I read them again. Then I pulled out my iPod, and I listened to those healing songs that I'd downloaded. I armed myself with spiritual weapons, and after a while I felt my body relax. Neville reluctantly crept away. Hope conquered Fear.

I don't want you to avoid online support groups based on what I've just written. They can be a lifesaver for some women. However, and this is important— you have to be careful not to allow yourself to get pulled into a state of "cyberchondria" by reading about the symptoms, treatment, and prognosis of others!! Notice those two exclamation points, and read that sentence again.

Every cancer story is unique, just like each of us is unique, and the only One who knows your story's ending is God. If you go online and find yourself coming away from a group feeling more worried and unsure, then it's time to find a new group. There are some wonderful ones out there, but you might have to dig a little to find the one that's right for you.

Before iGoogle went away in 2013, I used it as the home page on my laptop. I liked it because I could customize the way the page looked. iGoogle had all sorts of neat gadgets to dress up its page: news, weather, calendars, sports scores, movie reviews, and so much more. One of my favorite gadgets was the Bible Verse of the Day. I had it at the top center of my page so it's the first thing I saw when I logged on in the morning.

Following the bible verse, there was a tagline that read, "Leave a prayer request or a prayer." I didn't notice it until that day when I was reading messages in the cancer forum. Lord knows that I needed prayers, so I clicked on the link, and it took me to a registration page. There I typed in a username and set up a password. I entered my email address, clicked on "Register," and the screen refreshed.

"Change my heart oh God. Please I need you. Make me the woman You want me to be... Be with me always Lord. Guide me and give me wisdom. Amen."

"Dear Lord, Please keep my mother in your loving arms while she undergoes her lengthy stress test today. Thank you! Amen."

"Please, friends, help me pray for a new job opportunity and a difficult financial situation."

Each entry had more than a dozen responses, all of them encouraging and supportive, like these:

"Joining you in prayer for wisdom and guidance. God is good."

"Praying for your mother. What time is her test?"

"Agreeing with you in prayer for a new job and relief from your financial stress."

As I read the prayers and responses, I remembered that in Matthew 18:20, Jesus said, "For where two or three gather in my name, there I am with them." I supposed that also applied in cyberspace. So, I typed in my own prayer request: *I was diagnosed today with uterine cancer. Having surgery on Monday, and I'd appreciate your prayers.*

By that evening, more than twenty people had promised to pray for me. God didn't just send Aaron and Hur, He sent a whole platoon of soldiers! I got responses like:

"I'm adding you to my prayer list."

"Keep us posted. We care."

"Praying for you right now and every day for complete healing."

For most of my life, I've lived under the false pretense that more is better. If you spent a little time with me, you'd hear me say the words: "I want to make sure." It's that whole absolutes and certainties thing again. I want to make sure that I have enough. I want to make sure that I've locked all the doors. I want to make sure that every word is spelled right and that I didn't accidentally write "two" instead of "too." I want to make sure that everything is done on time and that everything is perfect. When those twenty-plus people agreed to pray for me, I searched for twenty more.

I Googled "Leave a prayer request," and I copied and pasted my prayer wherever I could. *I was diagnosed today with uterine cancer. Having surgery on Monday. I'd appreciate your prayers.* Most of the time I didn't get a personal response, but when I did it was like God's army marching into my camp.

I felt such comfort when I received an email from Ginger, the Prayer Team Director at Girlfriends in God. Along with a personal prayer and some appropriate scripture references, she wrote: *Jean, we are very sorry to hear about your cancer diagnosis, but you are not alone. We care about you and will pray for your healing. Please let us know how you are doing. Keep in touch!* YOU ARE NOT ALONE. Those four words sunk into my heart and settled there.

Aloneness is an integral part of the cancer journey. As hard as a cancer patient fights against it, loneliness sometimes leaks into that desire to stay positive and focused on a cure. Friends and family support us, but the truth is that the tumors are ours and ours alone. I found solace in Ginger's words, and I believed with all of my heart that she and her prayer team would pray for me. I saved her email address to my address book knowing that I would contact her again.

And then there were books. I'm accustomed to finding books between my front doors. Sometimes they come in packages—books I've ordered for my own enjoyment, samples of books I've written, or reference books from clients for me to use when I work on their projects. Sometimes books just show up, raw and without wrapping, left there by friends. So, I wasn't surprised to discover Pete Wilson's book, *Plan B (What Do You Do When God Doesn't' Show Up The Way You Thought He Would?)* in a thick, brown paper envelope between my front doors. I was, however, surprised by who had sent it. A cheery-looking note card was tucked inside.

"Hello, Dear Friend.
This book has blessed me through some difficult times, and I pray that it will help you, too.
Much Love,
Robin"

Robin is a Facebook friend, a friend whom I've never spoken with or laid eyes on, yet she'd taken time to mail me a book, a guide to getting me through the valley.

I remembered Karen's words, years before, as she gestured toward the patrons in Wilson's Coffee and Tea: "These are real people. You don't know who you're talking with when you're online." But I did know who I was talking with online. Robin and Ginger were more real to me than any of the strangers sipping cappuccinos and lattes in Wilson's Coffee and Tea. They were in every sense my friends, and they cared about me. And there were even more cyber friends who cared. God sent me a Social Media Army led by Susan, Renae, Shari, and Vicki. They frequently emailed personal messages of encouragement, and if a day went by and I didn't post to my Facebook status or Twitter page, surely one of them would write to ask me, "Is everything okay? I miss you." I formed bonds with these women, and I learned of their own struggles and needs for prayer. Together, we held up each other's hands as they supported me in my illness and I prayed for them in return. I didn't know it then, but later when I would lay in my hospital bed coming out of the anesthetic from my hysterectomy, one of the first things I'd ask of Sarah was to send a message to my online friends to let them know that I was okay. My laptop would be at the hospital with me, and as soon as my brain and fingers functioned again, I'd send a note to my cyber soldiers: *Pray that the pathology report shows no more cancer*. I knew that they would.

God moves in mysterious ways. Who coined that phrase anyway? It's not in the bible. Actually, it's attributed to an eighteenth century English poet and hymn writer named William Cowper. In his poem "Light Shining out of Darkness," he writes:

"God moves in a mysterious way,
His wonders to perform;
He plants his footsteps in the sea,
And rides upon the storm."

Nothing is nearer the truth. God does indeed have a mysterious way of doing things, and that is most apparent during the storms in our lives.

Such was the case when I Googled the words *uterine cancer* and *Madison, Wisconsin*. I had hoped to find information posted by the University of Wisconsin Hospital about my form of cancer. But instead, at the top of the results list I saw "Garden of Hope," an article from the *Wisconsin State Journal*. I clicked on it for no other reason than I am a gardener and it was spring, the time when every gardener's mind turns toward roughing up the earth. There, on the front page, looking out at me from a sea of blue phlox and yellow prairie buttercups, I saw—Sally!

Sally and I go all the way back to high school. She had been a senior, two years older than me, and I had looked up to her as if she were the big sister I always wanted but never had. She was patient enough to willingly guide me through my awkward and geeky sophomore year. The school band was our common ground. We both played flute and piccolo there, and Sally was our section leader. I aspired to take her place after she graduated. In fact, I aspired to be just like Sally in high school. Back then she was my idol, like Sandra Dee and Hayley Mills.

And there she was, Sally, forty years later, and on the front page of the *Wisconsin State Journal*. She looked a little bit older, but she still had her trademark perky smile and short, naturally-curly blond hair. The article started with the header: SOMETIMES, STORM CLOUDS DO HAVE SILVER LININGS. It went on to tell about Sally's uterine cancer diagnosis, that she had beaten her cancer, and how she had used photos of her beautiful flower garden to create a pamphlet and web site about uterine cancer awareness.

What made this encounter so mysterious is that I hadn't seen or spoken with Sally since 1968. I had no idea the path she had taken in life or that she had married and moved to a city more than a hundred miles away from me. I didn't know that three years earlier she had experienced the same symptoms that I'd had, nor that her cancer, like mine, was adenocarcinoma, well-differentiated, grade 1. And I certainly didn't know that God would use our shared interest in flower gardens to bring us together at this critical time in my life. But He did! And how amazing is that?

I found Sally's pamphlet online, and I saw that it included a contact form. *Sally,* I wrote, *do you remember me? Jean Fischer from high school. I have uterine cancer, too!* And, so, via cyber space, God added Sally as a soldier in my ever-growing army of supporters.

Whether in cyberspace or the real world, God sends His soldiers into battle exactly when needed. I believed this without a doubt because I had seen it happen before. During my mother's illness and also my dad's, helpers showed up at their God-appointed time. Sometimes they met a physical need, but more often they brought help for the soul, and their presence was truly miraculous.

My aunt and uncle had come from Texas to visit my mother at the hospital when she was dying. As they packed for their trip home, my uncle suffered a severe asthma attack that sent him to the hospital where he stayed for several days. It was meant to be. While my uncle was in the hospital, my mother's condition worsened, and her only sister was able to be at her bedside. Had it not been for that asthma attack, my aunt and uncle would have been well on their way back to Texas when my mother went to heaven.

My father's passing came with another well-timed miracle. I've told you that Dad spent many years in a nursing home slowly dying from Alzheimer's disease. Near the end, he was confined to his bed and in a perpetual light coma. During that time, I visited him every day, always in the morning. I'd sit next to his bed for a while and hold his hand. Sometimes his eyes would open and he'd look at me, but I know that he didn't recognize me. His condition didn't change much. He rested peacefully, and only God knew when the end would come.

I sat in my home office on the afternoon of April 4, 2008, working on a writing project, when God nudged me. The mild spring day neared its sunset, and I decided to stop my work and enjoy the last hour or so of daylight. Although I had rarely made the half-hour drive to visit my dad at suppertime, I did that day. I had been at the nursing home in the morning, but for no good reason I made the drive again, just to get out a little and enjoy the nice weather. When I got to Dad's room, I found him actively dying. This time, I was God's soldier arriving at the appointed time. Dad sat up and looked at me. I saw recognition in his eyes, and he struggled to say my name. It was the first time in more than a year that he knew who I was.

"It's okay, Dad," I told him. "God is sending Mom for you, and I'll wait here with you until she comes."

My father smiled at me, and then he settled back onto the pillows. Two hours later, God took Dad home, and I was there to see him off.

Whenever we ask the Lord to send help, He garners his soldiers in heaven and here on Earth. Sometimes, they're aware of their mission, but most often they enter the battle not knowing that they are soldiers in God's army. God sets the appointed time and place. The mission is His.

And so, when I faced battling Cancer alone, helpers arrived unaware—soldiers sent through cyberspace.

CHAPTER 13
Hysterectomy

"I lay in the bed at the hospital and said, 'let's see what I have left.' And I could see, I could speak, I could think, I could read. I simply tabulated my blessings, and that gave me a start."
—Dale Evans Rogers

    Monday morning arrived in a veil of gray clouds. A light drizzle fell, but I hardly noticed. I'd been busy packing my hospital bag and making sure that my house was in order and ready for my recovery. Doctor Z. had said the surgery would be laparoscopic, meaning that instead of cutting open my abdomen, he would make three small incisions, one at the base of my belly button and two near my hipbones. My reproductive organs would then be removed vaginally, and the top of the vagina sewn closed with sutures placed through the laparoscope. After spending one night in the hospital, I could go home to recover. There was the possibility of complications, and in that case I would need a total abdominal hysterectomy (TAH) so I planned for that just to be on the safe side.
    I knew that I could be restricted from driving for at least a few weeks, and it would be six weeks or more before I could do any lifting or anything physically active. So, I stocked my kitchen cabinets and refrigerator and freezer with easy to prepare food. I

thoroughly cleaned the house, did the laundry, and remade my bed with fresh linens. Then, I put a folded blanket and pillow on the living room sofa. I expected that I'd be spending a lot of time there when I got home. Finally, I made a list for a family member in the event that I didn't make it through the surgery. Like I've told you, my mantra is always "make sure," and it was remotely possible, although not probable, that I might not come home again. I wanted to make sure that everything was done right and that my affairs were in order.

Surprisingly, I felt calm. Or perhaps I was frozen. I don't know for sure. Still, by the grace of God, I readied for the hospital with that sense of peace mentioned in Philippians 4:7. "And the peace of God, which transcends all understanding, will guard your hearts and your minds in Christ Jesus."

Sarah arrived to drive me to the hospital. We chatted about nothing in particular until she parked her car in the hospital's parking ramp. Then we hardly talked at all as we made the long walk to the surgical floor, Five Palmer. As we traveled across the skywalk and down a wide hallway toward the bank of elevators, I remembered making that same walk with my mother eleven years before.

My surgery was scheduled for noon. I knew the drill. Preparation would be much the same as when I arrived for the D&C.

After I'd checked in, a nurses' aide led me to the changing area and told me to put on a hospital gown, a robe, and another pair of the blue slipper socks with white, rubber treads. She handed me a key to one of the metal lockers and told me to leave my clothing in there and return the key to her. And, oh, if I needed to use the bathroom, I should do that, too. I did all those things, and then I headed back to the pre-op area and a cot in one of the curtained cubbies.

A vague awareness accompanied me that this was the best I would feel for a long time. Mingled in were thoughts about my yard and garden. I had prepared for everything but that. My perennial flowers would grow while I recovered and so would the lawn. They would need tending. And my little garden pond stocked with goldfish had gone without its spring cleanup. All of these things were out of my control now. My helpers would take over their care. This left me with an uneasy feeling in the pit of my stomach. Turning over control is a process that I struggle with. Not only turning control over to people, but also to God.

I snuggled in under the sheet and thin blanket on the cot. A nurse came to start an IV, and when she went to put the needle into the back of my right hand, I stopped her. Somehow I knew that I'd be living with that needle and its long tube for a while, and I was right handed.

"Would it be a problem to put it in my left hand?" I asked her.

"Not at all," she said cheerfully. "We want you to be comfortable." She swabbed a cold liquid on the back of my hand to numb the pain. "Here's a little prick."

I barely noticed as the needle pierced the thin flesh and went into a vein.

An aide showed up in my cubby and announced that my surgery time had been moved up. The doctor was ready for me, now. After that, things happened quickly. Sarah was allowed into the cubby. So was a hospital chaplain who prayed with us both. Then Doctor Z. peeked in, dressed in his surgical scrubs. He gave me a thumbs up.

"I've just had lunch, and I'm ready to go," he said.

I heard my stomach growl. I hadn't eaten anything since the evening before, and afterward I'd done the required bowel cleansing routine. I was hungry for a cheeseburger—a double cheeseburger from Kewpee's, a favorite burger place in town.

Shortly after Doctor Z. left, my anesthesiologist arrived. I asked him for anti-nausea medication for when I came out of surgery. I had been nauseous on the way home after my D&C, and I didn't want to go through that again. He ordered a patch to be placed behind my ear, something with time-released medication, and the nurse hurried off to get it.

"You take good care of me," I told him, forcing a nervous smile.

"I will," he promised. "You can count on it."

Then he wiggled my big toe just like Doctor K., the anesthesiologist for my D&C, had. I wondered if it were a part of an anesthesiologist's training to learn to wiggle the big toe when reassuring a patient.

A flurry of activity surrounded me now as two nurses prepared me for surgery. While one nurse placed the patch behind my right ear and injected something into my IV, another struggled to get me into a pair of TED hose.

If you've never had to wear TEDs, then let me describe them to you. TEDs are lovely, thigh-high, white elastic stockings that patients wear to prevent blood clots. They fit very tight and feel amazingly good once they're on; however, getting them on is a process. When you're almost in a medically induced coma and a medical professional is working hard to get you into a pair of TEDs, you feel like you're jumping on a trampoline while flat on your back. As the nurse pushed the TEDs up over my knees and pushed and pushed again to get them onto my thighs, I felt the top of my head bump hard against the bed's headboard. I didn't care. I was rapidly falling asleep.

"Ouch!" the nurse said. "Sorry about that."

Sarah reached over and removed my glasses. "I'll hang onto these until you get settled in your room." She gave my hand a little squeeze. "Don't worry. It'll be fine." Déjà vu. Only this time, she leaned in, kissed my forehead and said, "We love you."

I woke up in the recovery room more than four hours later. I know, because my head was turned to the left, and I saw the clock on the wall. Something wasn't right. The doctor had said my surgery would take about an hour and a half. Either I had been very slow coming out of the anesthetic, or there had been complications. I managed to push far enough through the heavy fog to assess how I felt. Did I have any pain? No. Was I breathing on my own? Yes. Was I thinking? Yes. Could I see and hear? Yes. I wiggled my fingers and toes to find out if they still worked. They did.

A nurse sat at my bedside, but this time there were no ice chips. She swabbed my forehead with a cool washcloth. After my D&C, the first word I'd spoken was "Cancer?" That question had already been answered. I had cancer. Now I wondered how bad it was. I took a deep breath and forced out the word—

"Abdominal?"

My voice sounded too loud. Had I shouted?

"Abdominal?" I said it again trying to be quieter.

"Yes. You had abdominal surgery," the nurse answered.

I didn't respond. I lay there sinking into numbness. I began to comprehend that there had been complications and the doctor had cut me open. I should only have three small cuts in my belly, but instead I had an eight-inch-long vertical incision. I should have been out of recovery hours ago, but I still lay there. I wondered why I didn't hurt. How long would I be in the hospital? Would I need chemo and radiation? Would my hair fall out? Would I live? I drifted in and out of anesthesia, once in awhile catching a word or two of conversations in the recovery room. Some were about medical issues and others light-hearted chatter about husbands and wives, children and everyday life. The words swirled around in my head, and my brain struggled to tie them together into meaningful thoughts. It failed. I drifted off to sleep and my thoughts wove themselves into a peculiar dream.

In the dream, Bambi's mother was alive. If you've seen the classic animated Disney film, then you know that a hunter shot and killed Bambi's mother, a beautiful doe with soft, brown eyes, but she was very much alive in my post-op stupor. I had ambled through a tangled anesthetic maze and arrived in Cartoon Land where I romped with Bambi. Thumper the Rabbit was there, too, and so was Flower the Skunk. Thumper sat in the tall grass, retching.

"I think he's got a hairball," Flower suggested, reclining in the garden under a cloudless, blue sky.

I doubted it. I owned two cats, and I knew what a hairball sounded like.

A burst of cool air swept across my face, and something brushed through the hair on the top of my head. I ducked. A fat, great-horned owl landed near me on a low-hanging oak branch. The branch swung up and down making the owl look like it was bouncing on a pogo stick.

"He doesn't have a hairball. He's twitterpated," the owl proclaimed.

"Twitterpated?" asked Bambi. He gave his mother a quizzical look. "Does that have something to do with a bowel movement?"

Then all of them looked at me.

"Twitterpated! Surely you know what it means!"

They shouted it at me and in unison. Suddenly, I felt myself shrinking like Alice in Wonderland when she drank the potion in Lewis Carroll's story. What would my colorful, two-dimensional companions do to me if I gave them an unacceptable answer? I heard myself shouting back at them.

"Twitterpated! It means spending too much time on Twitter. You know? The Internet?"

I can only hope that I didn't shout it in my sleep. If I did, then I'd like to add a disclaimer to anyone who heard me that my dream wasn't all that unusual given that I've spent most of my life as a children's books author.

The next thing that I remember is waking up in my hospital room. I looked out the windows and decided it was either dusk or dawn. I wasn't sure. The clock said seven fifteen. AM or PM?

"Hello. Are you awake?" I heard Sarah's sympathetic voice. "Are you in any pain?"

She and her husband, Chuck, stood at my bedside.

I thought of the words from Psalm 91:11. "For (God) will command his angels concerning you to guard you in all your ways." When my mother was dying, my cousins Susie and Eileen and I stood near her bed. "I see three angels standing at the foot of my bed," Mom said. Now, I saw angels standing at the foot of mine—angel-helpers sent from God.

"No," I answered Sarah's question. "I'm not in pain." I decided it was evening. "Have you had supper?"

"We ate," Chuck answered. "Don't worry. We had something in the cafeteria."

Sarah's husband is a gentle and caring man, a medical professional at a hospital in a city not far from where I live. I felt relieved to see him there with Sarah. I trusted him, and I knew that he would be truthful with me about my surgery and the prognosis. During the next few minutes, I bombarded the poor man with more questions than I'm sure he wanted to answer.

"Why abdominal?" I asked.

He explained that Doctor Z. had performed the surgery laparoscopically, but then Pathology called while I was still on the operating table. My tumor was bigger than suspected and positioned at an odd angle. The part visible during surgery appeared like the tip of an iceberg. Its bulk and length were hidden in the tissue, and it had grown into the uterine wall, the thick muscle of the uterus. The doctor decided then to make an abdominal incision to harvest lymph nodes and look for signs that the cancer might have spread elsewhere in my pelvic region. That's why my surgery had taken so long. There wouldn't be any concrete answers until the pathology report came back.

More waiting. From what I was able to discern, my cancer remained grade one, adenocarcinoma, well-differentiated. Good news.

"What stage was it?" I asked Chuck. I tried to focus my thoughts on everything I'd read about staging. Doctor Z. had removed a cervical polyp during my D&C., and I had done enough research to know that stage 2 uterine cancer involved the cervix. Had my cancer spread that far? "If it spread, wouldn't that have shown up on the pathology report?"

I might have asked Chuck more than once. I had no idea what I was asking. I just remembered what I'd read online.

"We don't know anything yet," he hedged. "We won't know until the report comes back."

Sarah moved closer to my bed, or perhaps my eyes were just starting to focus on her.

"The next few weeks are going to be hard," she told me. "But we'll help you. Are you sure you're not in any pain?"

I wasn't. Doctor Z. and his team had done a great job with pain management. A small pump filled with a local anesthetic was attached to a thin tube placed into the incision during surgery. It would deliver anesthesia directly to the surgical site at a very low rate for several days. I also had a patient-administered IV, a larger pump connected to my IV, which contained morphine. The pump was set for a maximum dose per hour, and by pushing a button I could administer a measured quantity whenever I needed it.

"Don't be afraid to use that," Chuck reminded me. But during my hospital stay I pushed the button only a few times.

A nurse arrived in my room to check my blood pressure, measure my pulse oxygen, and take my temperature. This evaluation of my vital signs was the first of many, at least three times a day, for as long as I remained in the hospital.

"You're doing great!' the nurse said. "Can I get you anything?"

"Water," I begged. My mouth felt like it were stuffed with cotton. "I'm really thirsty."

"I'm sorry," she answered sympathetically, "but you can't have anything to eat or drink until your bowels and kidneys start working normally again. I can bring you some water and a swab, though."

A swab?

She returned with a cup filled with ice water. Inside the plastic cup was something that looked like a thin wooden skewer with a marble-sized foam ball attached to its bottom.

"You can run the swab across your lips," my nurse said. "And if you swallow a few drops of water, that's okay. But we don't want you to drink anything just yet."

Sarah smiled and handed me the swab. "Everything inside has to heal and get back to normal," she agreed. "And you need to rest now."

"And you do, too," I answered. Poor Sarah had been at the hospital with me since early morning. "You guys go home now. Oh, and when you get there, would you send a message to a few of my Facebook friends and tell them that I'm okay?"

I gave Sarah the names of my friends, and she wrote them down on a scrap of paper. She tucked the paper into her purse and then gave my hand a tight squeeze.

"It's going to be all right," she said.

I vaguely recall holding Sarah's hand and mumbling something about sisterhood and gratefulness. At least I hope that I told Sarah how grateful I was that she had been my angel that day. I don't remember much else about that evening. By the time Sarah and Chuck left my hospital room, I had slipped back into the fog.

CHAPTER 14
Healed!

Were you the sort of kid who waited patiently for Christmas to come? I wasn't. I confess that even before the Thanksgiving turkey carcass was simmering in Grandma's stockpot, I plotted to find out what my parents were getting me for Christmas. As the big day grew near, I couldn't wait for Mom and Dad to go out for an evening so Grandma Lily would baby-sit me. While she got busy with chores, I prowled through the house looking for my gifts. Mom suspected my sneakiness, so as soon as she bought a gift for me and before she hid it, she wrapped it. Mom liked tissue paper wrapping, and I liked it, too. If it was light-colored, all I had to do was hold it up to the light, press down on the paper, and voilà, I could see the package inside. No waiting patiently for me. I wanted to know with absolute certainty what I'd find under the tree on Christmas morning.

I'm embarrassed to say that I haven't changed. Confined to my hospital room after my surgery, I waited impatiently for the pathology report.

My first night in the hospital, I awoke to the sound of a man's voice shouting at me.

"Jean? .... *Jean!*"

I lurched into a sitting position. A searing pain tore down my belly along the fresh incision. At the same time, the hulking figure next to my bed grabbed onto my shoulders and held me there. I heard myself scream.

"Whoa! Hey, it's okay."

In the dimly lit room, I recognized that the intruder was a male nurse.

"It's okay. It's okay," he repeated several times, still holding me in a sitting position. "You're in the hospital. You had surgery."

I think I'd scared him as much as he'd scared me.

"You were sleeping so soundly that I couldn't wake you up. I have to take your vitals." He helped me to settle back onto the pillows. "You can't move fast like that," he said. "Take it nice and slow."

I probably wouldn't have moved at all had I not been terrified when he shouted trying to wake me. While he wrapped the blood-pressure cuff around my upper arm, I remembered that I'd had major surgery only a few hours before. Cancer.

"Is the pathology report back yet?" I asked.

He tightened the cuff until it hurt. "I don't know," he answered. "You'll have to wait and ask your doctor."

I heard the whoosh of air escaping as the blood pressure cuff loosened. "Well, where is he?" I asked.

The nurse checked a bag attached to the IV stand. "Where is who? You haven't used any of your pain medication. Don't be afraid to push the button. We want you to be comfortable."

"I'm not in pain," I told him. He looked at me skeptically. "Where is Doctor Z.?"

"He's at home," said the nurse, "It's past midnight. Why? Is something bothering you? Does anything hurt?"

Why couldn't I get through to this man? Didn't he know that I needed the results of that pathology report?

"No, nothing hurts," I told him. "The pathology report! I'm wondering what it said."

The nurse clipped something that looked like a clothespin onto my finger and mumbled about measuring my pulse ox.

"It takes a while for the pathology to come back," he offered. "You rest now." He removed the device from my finger and patted my shoulder. "Should I leave the light on?"

"But how long?" I pressed. "Wouldn't they know right away

if the results were bad?"

The nurse moved the tray table nearer my bed. "You can ask your doctor in the morning," he said. "Do you want me to close the door a little so you can sleep? Can I get you anything?"

All I wanted was that pathology report. I wanted it the same way I wanted to press down on the tissue paper at Christmas and see that the package inside held exactly what I'd asked for. But this time, the package was wrapped up so tight and it was so well hidden that I had to wait. *But they that wait upon the LORD shall renew their strength; they shall mount up with wings as eagles; they shall run, and not be weary; and they shall walk, and not faint.* Isaiah 40:31. (KJV)

The Woman With The Issue Of Blood waited upon the Lord. She waited for twelve years. She waited while she searched for a doctor who could heal her. She waited for countless treatments to work. She waited for Jesus. She waited for that precise moment when their paths would cross and she could touch his cloak. She waited, and most likely she learned patience as one failed attempt at healing her disease led to another.

In Luke Chapter 8, we find out that while The Woman With The Issue Of Blood waited, Jesus traveled from village to village teaching and working miracles. Word of His miracles spread quickly, and by the time He left for the next village or town, its residents expected him. Crowds gathered and waited for Him.

Now, I don't know about you, but I've never seen a crowd that waited patiently. Before a parade starts, people gather along the streets and, every once in a while, you'll see them glance in the direction that the parade is supposed to come from. "When is it going to get here?" little children ask. "I want it to start!" Or maybe you've been at a political event and waited for the key speaker to show up? I remember when President George W. Bush came to our town, and I, along with hundreds of others, sat on hard bleacher seats for hours waiting for his motorcade to arrive. "When is he coming? Why is he late?" Impatience.

While The Woman With The Issue Of Blood waited for Jesus to arrive, so did another man. His name was Jairus, and I doubt that he waited patiently. He had a need, an urgent one. Jairus' only daughter, a little girl just twelve years old, was dying. She was very near death, or perhaps she had already died and Jairus didn't know it because he had left home in such a hurry to seek help. This man he'd heard of called Jesus was has last and only hope.

We can assume that everyone in town knew Jairus, and they knew him well because he served as a leader in the local synagogue. It is important to point out here that some religious leaders weren't sure that Jesus was who He said He was—the Messiah, God's anointed king, the One who would save the Jews from their sins. Did Jairus believe it? We can't know. But desperation led him to hope that Jesus could heal his little girl. I imagine that he paced impatiently among the crowd waiting for Jesus to show up. And when Jesus did arrive, Jairus did something very unusual for a man of his position. He fell down at Jesus' feet and begged for help. "Please, Jesus! Come to my house right now! My little girl is dying!"

Jesus took Jarius' plight very seriously. He didn't wait, but He went right away with Jairus to his house. The bible says that a crowd went with them, a crowd so huge that it almost crushed Jesus. The people pushed against Him, shoving him along. Imagine an unruly mob lumbering down a narrow, dirt road, all of them anxious to see if Jesus could heal Jairus' daughter, all of them impatient to receive a miracle of their own. Surely, this huge crowd made it slow to travel. Jairus must have wished that they could move along more quickly, even run, to his house.

And then, Jesus stopped.

The crowd stopped with Him.

"Who touched Me?" He said turning around. "I know that power has gone out from Me."

"Not, me!"

"Not, me, either!"

"I didn't do it."

They all denied touching Him, and in the confusion Jairus was probably going crazy. He wanted to move on, to get home to his little girl.

But then, a haggard-looking woman, perhaps with blood on her cloak, fell down at Jesus' feet, much the same as Jairus, the synagogue leader, had fallen just minutes before.

"I touched you," she confessed, trembling in awe of Him.

Most likely, she shed tears of joy as she told him her story. She'd waited and waited for twelve years to be healed from her issue of blood, and no one could help her. But He— Jesus—had healed her! She knew it in her heart. She was sure of it, and she was grateful. So grateful. And while Jairus waited eagerly, listening to all this, Jesus waited patiently while the woman finished telling Him her story. Then, He encouraged her.

"Daughter," He said. "Your faith has healed you. Go in peace." Mark 5:34.

While The Woman With The Issue Of Blood was still there talking with Jesus, a man approached the crowd. Maybe no one noticed him except Jarius. The man had come from Jarius' house, and from the expression on the man's face Jarius could tell that the news wasn't good.

"Your daughter is dead," the man said. "Don't bother the Teacher anymore."

I imagine that when Jarius heard, he felt like my friend Linda did when her mother died of cancer—defeated and angry, or as Linda would say, "Ugly." If only you had moved faster, Jesus, Jairus might have thought. If only you had ignored this unclean woman. If only you had not spent so much time with her. . . then my little girl would be alive. Jairus must have experienced that horrible, hopeless feeling of being out of control.

If you have ever lost a loved one, you know what I mean. There comes that moment when you realize that you, the doctors, medical science, and technology have failed. There is nothing more that you can do to save the one you love. And then, if you're Christian, you pray. You turn to the Lord looking for a miracle, and if that isn't possible, then you ask Him to take away your fear, to comfort you and give you strength. When trapped in the darkness, you look for Hope.

"Don't be afraid," Jesus said to Jairus. "Just believe, and she will be healed."

Say what? Healed! The girl is dead.

I suppose that the crowd moved more slowly toward Jairus' house then. After all, the girl had passed away. No need to hurry. When they got there, they heard the people inside wailing and mourning for the child. They gathered around the front door, all of them wanting to go in to see what Jesus would do. It would take a miracle to bring Jairus' daughter back to life. Could He? Would He revive her?

Have you ever been in a crowd and witnessed a miracle? Probably not. Miracles don't often arrive with a crowd of people there watching. Instead miracles come softly and silently while we wait unaware that something wonderful is about to happen.

I was watching television on the morning of January, 8, 2011 when Congresswoman Gabrielle Giffords was shot at a supermarket in Tucson, Arizona. "Gabby," as she was readily known, had been outside the store, meeting informally with some of her constituents, when a young man carrying a pistol opened fire on the crowd. He walked up to Congresswoman Giffords and shot her, point blank, in the head. Horrible! The story rapidly unfolded, and cable news stations broadcast live video of the chaotic scene. Life flight helicopters landed and took off. One of them carried the congresswoman. Before long, the news came that Gabrielle Giffords had died. Those who heard the report that Saturday afternoon mourned her death and asked how this could have happened. Where was God? Why hadn't He stopped it? But then something unexpected occurred. The news stations rescinded their report that Giffords was dead. They began reporting that she was alive and in surgery. In the midst of a terrible tragedy where six people had died and many others were injured, there was hope that the congresswoman might live. And she did live! In the following days and weeks, Americans celebrated each small step that Gabby Giffords made toward recovery. A bullet had torn a path clear through her brain, but she lived and recovered. A miracle! While Americans watched the television believing that Congresswoman Giffords had died, Jesus entered the emergency room unnoticed. He touched Gabrielle Giffords and gave her life. Against all odds.

Jesus worked a similar miracle at Jairus' house. He refused to let the crowd go inside with him. He allowed only Jairus and his wife and three disciples, Peter, James, and John. The little girl lay unmoving in her bed. Jesus reached for her hand. He held it and He said to her, "My child, get up!" Then the little girl's spirit returned to her body. She lived!

Whether we wait patiently or impatiently, we know this: Jesus will show up. We might not always get what we ask for. There are times when we press down on the tissue paper and discover that what's under the wrapping isn't what we wanted. But, Jesus always knows what we need. And while we wait for him to answer our prayers, He teaches us about patience and faith.

I was too numb to pray while I waited for my pathology report. I relied on God's soldiers to do that for me. My thoughts turned away from what I hoped for and toward renewing my strength. That first morning in the hospital, it became so important to me to get up out of my bed, put on some makeup, and sit in a chair.

"Look at you!" Sarah exclaimed when she came to visit me. I think she expected me to be lying in bed looking ashen and in pain.

Pastor John and his family arrived a short time later.

"Wow!" he said. "You're even wearing makeup."

I hoped that I'd put my lipstick on right and that I wasn't smiling at him wearing a Cover Girl Smokey Rose mustache.

I sat in the chair in my room, and I looked at my disheveled hospital bed. I didn't want to go back to it. If I felt really tired I would, but I wasn't tired, not in my spirit anyhow. I knew that whatever the pathology report showed, Jesus was with me. I would be dishonest if I told you that I wasn't at all afraid. I had my moments of terror. But they passed swiftly, and solely because of God's mercy and grace.

When Doctor Z. showed up that morning, he said it could take a couple of days for the report to come back. More waiting. I asked what he thought. Had the cancer spread? He dodged my question. I asked him when I could drink something and eat. (I still had that Kewpee's cheeseburger on my mind.) The doctor said not until my bowels woke up. After abdominal surgery, it takes time for a person's bowels to "kick in," he said. I couldn't eat until they showed signs of working. In other words, to put it delicately, until they passed gas.

While passing gas is something you rarely, if ever, talk about with strangers, it became the focus of the rest of my hospital stay. Periodically, a nurse would stick her head into my room and ask, "Have you passed gas yet?" On every shift when the nurses took my vital signs, they always asked the question. Tuesday went by. No gas. No food. I felt hungry, and I ached for a tall glass of something cold. But the swab and some lemon flavored lip balm were the only things on the menu. The lip balm made my hunger tolerable. I pretended that it was lemonade, lemon chicken, lemon meringue pie... On Wednesday morning, Doctor Z. made his rounds before breakfast.

"I hear that you haven't passed gas yet," he said. "You need to do that so you can start eating."

I felt embarrassed and somewhat perplexed. Usually you feel embarrassed when you do pass gas in public. But now I was embarrassed because I hadn't. He sat on the edge of my bed and explained how bowels work and the sounds they make. I listened politely, but impatiently. I couldn't care less about the function of my bowels. I wanted to hear that the cancer was gone.

When he finished his explanation I asked, "Do you have any news for me?"

"News?"

Come on. Certainly, he knew how anxious I felt to get the pathology report.

"The report!" I said. "Has it come back yet?"

"Oh, sure," he said straightening his gaudy blue and green bowtie. "Everything is fine."

I could have kissed him!

"Everything is fine? I'm cancer free? It's gone?"

"You're cancer free," he confirmed. "The nodes were clear, and there's nothing suspicious."

"What stage was it?" I asked. "Was it stage two?"

Doctor Z. stood up, took out a pen and scribbled something on my chart. "No. It's stage 1. I'm not certain if they'll call it 1B or 1C. I think, probably, 1B."

That wasn't good enough for me. I wanted absolutes and certainties. "Why don't you know?" I prodded.

The doctor picked up a notepad that I had on my tray table, and he made a rough sketch of a uterus.

"Your tumor was angled, like this." He drew an arrow in the uterus. "The tip of it was exactly halfway through the uterine wall. Less than a half, and it's stage 1B; more than a half, and it's 1C. So, we'll let the oncologist make that call."

I felt like I were on a football field waiting for the referee's decision. Bring out the tape. Is it a first down? A fraction of an inch makes all the difference. My mind muddled with elation and a million questions, but I asked just one.

"What are the chances that it will come back?"

He put the notepad back on the table. "Statistically, around six percent," he told me. "Usually if it does come back, it's in the vaginal cuff, the place at the top of the vagina that we've sewn shut. But, you're fine right now. You shouldn't worry."

He promised to let me celebrate the good news with some clear broth, but no solid food.

Wednesday passed with no sign of gas. By Thursday, I was starving. Along with clear broth and water, the doctor allowed me to have flavored gelatin. I gobbled it down enjoying every bite like it were a Christmas dinner with all the trimmings. Then things started to happen. I got gas pains. Bad ones. They were so bad that I used the morphine drip to control the pain. Every time the nurses made their rounds, they listened to my stomach with their stethoscopes.

"Something's happening in there," the night nurse said joyfully. "There's gas in there. I can hear it gurgling."

I heard it, too, and I felt it. "Did anyone tell you my good news?" I asked.

"No, Honey," she said still listening to my bowel sounds. "What's your good news?"

"I'm cancer free!" I grinned and gave her a thumbs up.

"That's wonderful," she said, with not as much enthusiasm as I would have liked. She pushed the stethoscope firmly against my belly. "Now, if we can just get you to pass gas, that'll be really good news."

Really good news! Being cancer free wasn't really good news? To me, compared to beating cancer, passing gas was like winning a dollar on a multi-million lottery ticket. However, my nurse had her priorities. Gas.

The next morning, when the dayshift nurses arrived, they got the news that my bowels had rumbled and growled until finally enough gas had built up to be expelled. They came to my room and clapped for me, and they promised I could eat whatever I wanted for breakfast.

My waiting had ended, not only waiting for a good, solid meal, but also waiting to be healed of my cancer. I had waited for the Lord to answer my prayers, sometimes patiently and often not, and He had. The cancer hadn't been taken from my body the way that I had expected, instantaneously like the way Jesus had healed The Woman With The Issue Of Blood, but I left the hospital thinking that I would run again without Cancer making me weary, and that I would walk in faith knowing that Cancer had lost its grip on me. However God had done it, I had been healed!

A quick note, but an important one. The way that uterine cancer is staged has changed since my surgery. New research changes the ways that cancers are diagnosed and treated. If you or a loved one is facing any type of cancer, it is a good idea to check the American Cancer Society's web site, or another reputable source, for the latest information and statistics.

Reader's Notes—Part Two
Use this page to list ways that you might increase your own faith or encourage a loved one who is battling cancer.

Part Three – Facing The Future

CHAPTER 15
Toward Deliverance

"And lead us not into temptation, but deliver us from evil."
—Jesus, The Sermon on the Mount. (Matthew 6:13)

The bible tells us not to worry. Jesus is very clear about it: "Do not worry about tomorrow for tomorrow will worry about itself. Each day has enough troubles of its own." Matthew 6:34. Preachers preach about worry. Countless devotionals have been written about it, and still Christians worry. Are you one of them? I am. I confess that I'm a worrier. I know that my Heavenly Father will meet all of my needs. I have no reasons to doubt that. But I grew up in a family of worriers. Worry is in my DNA; it's in my blood.

The reality of my cancer didn't sink in until the day I came home from the hospital. There, while I rested on my sofa, it hit me. Oh, dear! I'd had cancer! In a two-week whirlwind, I'd experienced two surgeries, good news and bad news, and a five-day hospital stay. My tears finally thawed and I cried praising God for His healing and faithfulness. But then Neville showed up. He sat down on the end of my sofa, wearing his red velvet smoking jacket. After he took a long drag on the cigarette that he held in its black lacquer holder, he exhaled a cloud of dense, blue smoke directly into my face.

"There's a chance that your cancer could come back," he teased me. "You haven't had the best of luck lately. Maybe you'll be one of those who get it again."

As much as I wanted to push Neville's suggestions out of my head, I couldn't, and I still can't, not completely. I'm three years in remission now, and sometimes I worry that the cancer will come back.

Whenever Neville whispers to me about a recurrence, I hang onto the words of Isaiah 43:18-19. "Forget the former things; do not dwell on the past. See, I am doing a new thing! Now it springs up; do you not perceive it? I am making a way in the wilderness and streams in the wasteland."

Forgetting the former things is difficult for a cancer patient. However you look at it, cancer is life changing. It is nearly impossible to look back at how life used to be and not be astonished by how quickly things changed. I'm no exception. Some days my mind drifts back to the whys and skips ahead to the what ifs.

When my friend Linda learned that her mother had cancer, she asked why. She wanted an answer that would make sense to her, some sort of logical explanation that might help mend her brokenness. Linda attempted to fit the jagged pieces of her life together again neatly like a jigsaw puzzle, but she couldn't.

We humans often ask why when awful, unexpected things come at us. As much as we search for answers, we usually find none. We're left having to accept that bad things do happen, and most of the time we have no control over them.

If you are familiar with the Book of Job, you know that Job suffered. He suffered so miserably that his wife wished he would die and be freed from his agony. How did Job react to his situation? He asked the obvious question: Why me? He asked why me, yet he remained faithful. Job said that even if his suffering led to death, he would continue to hope in God. Instead of just dwelling on why God allowed him to suffer, Job faced suffering with the best positive attitude that he could garner.

When faced with horrendous misery, Job trusted God to deliver him from evil. The bible tells us that in this particular instance God allowed Job to suffer because He wanted to prove a point to Satan about Job's faithfulness.

But we can't always know the exact reason why God allows suffering into our lives. There are many theories about why bad things happen, but the full truth can't be known here on Earth. The bible says in 1 John 1:5, "God is light. In him there is no darkness at all." This is our assurance that there is nothing evil in God. He doesn't cause cancer or other evil things. But, for whatever reason, bad things do happen, and sometimes we face valleys, just as Job did.

Who created cancer? I believe it's our old friend, Neville. In 2 Corinthians 4:4, Paul calls Neville "the god of this age." It was true in Paul's time, and it's true now: since the fall of Adam and Eve in the Garden of Eden, Neville, or as he is commonly known, Satan, has roamed the earth doing evil things. In my opinion, cancer is born in evil; that's not to say in our own sinfulness, but at the root of all sin.

In Job's story, we discover some weapons that we can use to fight against Satan. These weapons are faith, trust, and hope. When we hang onto them, God delivers us from evil. Look around you, and you will find many examples of God's deliverance.

One of my favorites comes from the North American Bear Center in Ely, Minnesota. In January 2010, while 25,000 people watched, a web camera placed discreetly in a black bear's den broadcast live as she gave birth to a single cub. Lily and her cub, Hope, the names given them by researchers, captured the hearts of viewers. In the weeks that followed, their fans watched until Hope grew big enough to leave the den. When the little cub ventured out into the world, many worried. Would she survive in her dangerous surroundings? She was so small and vulnerable.

The North American Bear Center's mission is to learn more about the behavior of black bears in the wild. The researchers there track bears by using humane GPS radio collars. Lily wore a collar, but Hope did not. A collar would become too tight around her neck as she grew. The researchers relied on the signals sent from Lily's collar to know exactly where Lily and Hope were. Every day they posted updates on their web site and also on their Facebook page, and before long, more than 100,000 people had signed up to follow the adventures of Lily and Hope.

For a while, the pair traveled uneventfully through the woods together. Then, one day, when Hope was about twelve weeks old, something happened that changed everything. Lily ran off and left Hope alone. The frightened little bear cub scurried high into a tree where instinct told her that she would be safe. She waited there. Could Hope survive if Lily didn't come back? The researchers at the Bear Center waited and worried. They posted about the separation on Facebook, and some of the Facebook friends responded with prayers.

After a day or so, Hope climbed down from her perch. Not finding Lily anywhere nearby, she started walking. Something inside of the little cub told her not to give up. She needed to find her mother. Later, researchers would determine that Hope had navigated alone through dangerous territory, more than two miles around a lake, through swamps, across a stream, and into the dense forest. Finally, she arrived at a familiar spot where she had been with her mother two weeks before. There Hope waited faithfully for Lily to come back. The GPS system allowed researchers at the Bear Center to know exactly where Lily was, but Hope's location remained a mystery. For five days, the cub had been without her only source of food, her mother's milk, and they worried that she must be starving.

Enter Mike and Ellen, a couple who owned a cabin in Ely. They were out for a drive one afternoon when they saw Hope wandering at the side of a forest road. Both were well acquainted with the North American Bear Center, and they knew about the separation. Mike took out his cell phone, and he called the Center to report that Hope was alive.

As a rule, the researchers don't get in the way of nature's course, but this time they made an exception. Mike and Ellen kept track of Hope's whereabouts until someone from the Bear Center got there. Little Hope was loaded into a large pet carrier and transported to Lily less than a mile away. When Hope saw her mother she ran toward her bawling almost like a human child. If she could speak, Hope might have cried, "Mama! Mama! I was lost, but God delivered me from evil!"

Yea, though a walk through the valley of the shadow of death, I will fear no evil: for thou art with me . . . Lead us not into temptation, but deliver us from evil. You know those familiar scripture verses. They're found in Psalm 23 and also Matthew 6:13. They promise us God's presence and deliverance.

In the Gospel of Matthew, Jesus says: "Are not two sparrows sold for a penny? Yet not one of them will fall to the ground outside your Father's care." If God delivers sparrows and bear cubs from evil, then we know that He will do even more for us. "And even the very hairs on your head are all numbered," Jesus says. "So don't be afraid. You are worth more than many sparrows." Matthew 10:29-31. Jesus' words remind us that God delivers us from evil things, like cancer, when we hold tight to faith, trust and hope.

I think most cancer patients worry and are frightened that the cancer might come back. Maybe that idea isn't always foremost in their minds, but it's there, and it usually surfaces just before they go for their checkups.

The recovery from my hysterectomy took six weeks. While I healed, I wasn't too worried about the cancer returning. I focused instead on regaining my energy and strength. I made steady progress, and I celebrated each small step: driving, vacuuming, hauling groceries, and cutting the grass. By autumn, I felt much like my old self again. I had breezed through recovery better than expected, and I looked toward the future with hope—until October, about a week before the first of my every-three-month checkups with Doctor Z. That's when Neville returned.

"Be prepared," he warned me. "The pathologist might have missed something. You could still have cancer cells floating around somewhere in your body and not even know it. It doesn't mean anything that you feel good. You might not know that the cancer is back until you get really sick. They don't always find it right away."

I tried to fight against his worrisome, evil implications, but I failed. There were those absolutes and certainties attacking me again. My kind of cancer comes back in only six percent of cases, but I wanted to know without a doubt that I won't be in that six percent. Of course, that's not possible.

I worried myself through that first exam and also while waiting for the results. Finally, when Pam from the doctor's office called to say that everything was fine, I wept.

"Thank you, Jesus!"

I said it again and again, so grateful to Him that I remained cancer free. With every checkup I've had since then, I'm more positive, but Neville still nags at me about that six percent. I have to remind myself that God delivers us from evil!

I wonder how The Woman With The Issue Of Blood felt in the weeks and months following her healing. Did her joy dissolve into worry? Did she wonder if the cure would last? After countless trips to doctors and times when her bleeding must have stopped for a while, surely she questioned if she were truly healed of her disease. Was she like me? Even after Jesus healed her, did she have trust issues, and did she let the desire for absolutes and certainties veil her hopefulness?

Since I began writing this book, Linda's mother went to be with the Lord. At her funeral, I had a hard time holding back my tears. I don't often cry at funerals, I walk through them numb, but I cried at this one. My frozenness thawed that day. I didn't cry for Linda's mom. She had lived fully, loved and been loved, laughed and was blessed. She had fought cancer with courage and grace, and God had finally ended her suffering. But my heart ached for Linda. I knew how long and painful the cancer journey had been for my friend. Her mother's last days were filled with suffering, and Linda had shared in that suffering at her mother's bedside. Linda had faced her mom's cancer angry with God and without hope in His goodness. Worse, Neville had convinced her that she walked in the valley of her mother's cancer alone. That made me sad. I cried knowing that Linda was stuck in Evil's grip without faith, trust, and hope. Cancer had left its mark on my friend. Her wounds will take time to heal, but I believe with all of my heart that they will.

Cancer's scars aren't always invisible. Every day when I shower, I see what remains of the incision on my belly, and I remember that it's there because I had cancer. Sometimes, I avoid looking at it, and other times I try to celebrate it as a battle scar representing my victory over Evil.

My scar reminds me of the familiar story in the bible about Jesus' disciple Thomas. You might know him as Doubting Thomas. If you look up "doubting Thomas" in Webster's Dictionary, you'll find it defined: *an incredulous or habitually doubtful person.* Poor Thomas! His legacy is forever tied to hopelessness. But it isn't entirely true that he was habitually doubtful. Like the other disciples, Thomas faithfully followed Jesus believing that He was the Messiah who would save Israel.

The bible tells us that after Jesus' death, the disciples locked themselves into an Upper Room because they worried that the Jewish leaders would come after them. For whatever reason, Thomas wasn't with them. While he was away, Jesus appeared to the disciples. Hallelujah! He had risen from the dead, just as He had said He would. But Thomas missed seeing the risen Christ. By the time he arrived at the Upper Room, Jesus had gone away. Thomas, a man who liked facts, doubted that his friends had seen Jesus.

Thomas was a disciple who all along had questioned Jesus and looked for concrete answers. It must have frustrated him to no end when Christ spoke in parables. One day, when Jesus said that He was going to His Father's house to prepare a place for His disciples, Thomas asked for facts.

"Lord," he said, "we don't know where you are going. So how can we know the way?"

Thomas dealt in absolutes and certainties, and he couldn't fully believe anything Jesus said unless he saw it with his own eyes.

Jesus came again to the Upper Room, and this time Thomas was there. Did Thomas believe it when he saw Jesus standing in front of him? No. Jesus had to show Thomas his scars, the places where the nails had pierced his hands. Jesus had to invite Thomas to touch the wound in His side.

"Stop doubting and believe!" Jesus said to this disciple.

And that is Christ's message to all cancer survivors. Stop doubting and believe.

Are you like Thomas? I am. I hate to admit it, but so many

times I've said, "Jesus, I believe in you, but show me that you're there. Do something to give me hope that the cancer won't come back." Jesus' response to me is the same as his response to Thomas: "Because you have seen me, you have believed; blessed are those who have not seen and yet have believed." John 20:29.

We cancer patients sometimes wrestle with worrisome thoughts. When we're cancer free, doctors can't tell us for sure that the cancer won't recur. When the cancer is there, we don't know if treatment will cure us. None of us know our "expiration dates." Cancer is a disease where there are no absolutes and certainties, and that's what makes living with it so hard. But, if Jesus were here standing with us in the flesh, He might say, "Stop doubting and believe! Forget that the research says there is a 6%, 20%, 50%, or 80% chance of recurrence. Forget the former things that you've been told. I am doing a new thing! Look toward the future with hope."

Evil can so easily take hope away. At best, cancer can be cured or put into remission, sometimes forever. At worst, it comes like a perpetual thief stealing from its victims a little at a time until finally there's nothing left to take. Cancer patients might worry about whether they'll be able to endure the stress and suffering. But if you think about it, there isn't one cancer patient who didn't endure. We all endure the valleys in our lives. We endure them until we die. For some of us, that means long after we've survived cancer.

Evil can't conquer believers. If we beat Cancer, we beat Satan. If we don't beat Cancer, then we go to be with the Lord in heaven, a place where Satan can't touch us anymore. God will deliver us from evil. Does that mean that we won't suffer? No. But our Heavenly Father doesn't abandon us to cancer, or suffering, or any other evil thing.

In those times when coping with cancer is a struggle, we can follow the example of Hannah, another barren woman in the bible, this time in 1 Samuel. In her trouble, Hannah poured her heart out to God. "Lord, Almighty," she said. "If you will only look on your servant's misery and remember me." And God did remember Hannah. He heard her prayer for a child, and He answered by giving her a son. "My heart rejoices in the Lord,"

Hannah proclaimed, thanking Him for His mercy. "In the Lord my (strength) is lifted high. My mouth boasts over my enemies for I delight in your deliverance." 1 Samuel 2:1.

When we meet worry and doubt with faith and hope, we take the first step in moving beyond cancer toward deliverance. God looks on us in our misery, and He remembers us. He gives us the strength to endure. In Him we trust, we hope, and we persevere.

CHAPTER 16
Into The Light

My cancer didn't end with the hysterectomy. I had decisions to make about my aftercare. I had beaten Cancer, but I faced the possibility that it could come back, a slim possibility but a possibility nonetheless. At my first post-surgery checkup, a week after I left the hospital, Doctor Z. explained that my kind of cancer wouldn't require follow-up chemotherapy; however, he suggested that I consider preventative radiation therapy. I hadn't thought that I'd need anything other than regular checkups, so the idea of radiation took me by surprise. Doctor Z. referred me to a radiology oncologist to discuss preventative treatment options, and an appointment was set for the following week.

I turned again to the Internet for information. What I found there led me into a confusing maze with no clear way out. As I muddled my way through a plethora of abstracts from medical journals, I discovered that some clinical trials advocated radiation as a preventative option for women with my kind of cancer—adenocarcinoma, well-differentiated, grade 1, stage 1B or 1C—but those were older studies. The newer trials showed little difference in long-term survival among women who had received radiation therapy and those who had not. To further complicate things, I learned that the system of staging endometrial cancer had recently changed. With the newer method, Stage 1C didn't exist anymore.

The new system indicated that if the cancer had grown more than halfway through the myometrium, it was Stage 1B. Less than one-half was Stage 1A. I turned to the American Cancer Society's web site looking for treatment recommendations. I found general treatment information there but no concrete recommendation for my kind of cancer. Their page included a disclaimer stressing the importance of the patient making a decision with her doctor. It also suggested that the patient might want to get a second opinion. I left my research feeling perplexed.

Years ago when I worked as an editor at Golden Books, I had the task of creating children's puzzle books that included mazes. My job was to decide on the shape of the maze and its complexity. Then, I passed my instructions along to an illustrator who drew the maze and afterward returned it to me for checking. The goal was a perfect labyrinth, one that had only one path from any point in the maze to any other point, no inaccessible sections, no circular paths, no open areas. By starting at the beginning and being careful not to choose lanes that led to dead ends, I could easily negotiate from the maze entrance to its exit. A perfect maze is a no-brainer. You don't have to choose the best path to reach the end, because there is only one correct path. Once you find it, you're home free.

Oh, if only life were that easy! When I searched for information about post-cancer preventative treatment, or "adjuvant therapy" as it's called, I found myself stuck in a non-perfect maze, one with endless circular paths and plenty of open spaces.

So far on my cancer journey, I had escaped interacting with other cancer patients. I hadn't been on the oncology wing during my hospital stay, and since my hysterectomy had left me cancer free, I hadn't been approached by the hospital's social workers regarding cancer patient support. Everything had happened to me so fast that I didn't think of myself as a cancer patient. That I was one didn't sink in until I arrived at the cancer treatment center for my appointment with Doctor U., the radiology oncologist.

As I approached the entrance, I met a middle-aged woman in a motorized wheelchair. I hurried on ahead of her planning to open the door so she could get in.

"Don't worry about it, Honey," she said. "It'll open by itself."

This gaunt woman, wearing a short-sleeved sundress, flashed a wide smile. I noticed how white her teeth were against her golden yellow skin.

"So what are you in for?" she asked as we went together through the wide double doors.

Her question made me feel like a convicted criminal about to be processed and thrown into prison.

"Nothing yet," I told her. "I had uterine cancer. I'm here to find out if I need radiation."

I felt guilty as soon as the words left my mouth. The colorful tie-dyed scarf wrapped around the woman's head was evidence that she was there for chemotherapy. I felt embarrassed telling her that I'd *had* cancer, past tense.

"Radiation's a breeze compared to chemo," she offered as we headed toward the check-in desk. "But, hey, if you end up needing chemo, that's not so bad either. Whatever keeps you alive is good, right?"

She directed her question not only to me, but also toward about a half dozen people sitting on turquoise vinyl chairs in the sun-filled waiting area. None of them seemed to hear her.

"Right," I answered softly.

"By the way," she said when we reached the desk. "I'm Gail."

She stopped the wheelchair and extended her right hand in my direction. I grasped her boney fingers gently not wanting to hurt her. The black bruises on the back of her hand and on the inside fold of her elbow looked painful.

"Hi, Gail," I said. "I'm Jean."

Some of the people in the waiting area sat statue-like watching CNN on a television fixed to the wall. Others sat randomly thumbing through magazines, not really reading them. A few sat in wheelchairs staring into space and looking more like Gail than the others. The only conversation happening in the waiting area besides Gail's and mine was between Wolf Blitzer and James Carville on the television.

The lady at the reception desk seemed well acquainted with Gail.

"I see you're wearing your Tuesday scarf," she said. "You

know how much I love the Tuesday scarf."

"I know you love it," Gail quipped. "I'm leaving it to you in my will."

I winced.

"That's nice of you, Sweetie," said the receptionist. "But I don't want it for a long, long time."

"And I don't want you to have it for a long, long time," Gail answered, still flashing her radiant smile.

A nurses' aide arrived at the desk to accompany Gail to the treatment room. "Nice meeting, you, Jean," Gail said as she scooted away in her motorized chair. "Don't worry, you'll do just fine."

Proverbs 17:22 says, "A cheerful heart is good medicine, but a crushed spirit dries up the bones." I wondered: when I looked at Gail was I catching a glimpse of my future. And if this were my future, could I face it with a wide grin like hers and a positive attitude. I hoped so. God bless people like Gail who face their valleys with hope.

I filled out the necessary paperwork, and I returned it to the receptionist at the desk. She asked me to stand in front of a pale green screen on a nearby wall so she could take my picture.

"Why do you need a photograph?" I asked.

I hated having my picture taken. I have ever since those first-grade days when the kids called me "Plop." I'd never been photographed at a doctor's appointment before, and again I felt like I were being processed for a prison cell, this time a mug shot.

"We like to have a photo of you on file," she answered. "And, when you finish your treatment, then we'll put it on our Survivors' Board. Smile now."

I forced a diminutive smile, and she snapped my picture.

"Beautiful!" she exclaimed, showing me the image on the camera's LCD screen. I looked like a deer caught in the headlights.

Doctor U. entered the examining room like a flash of lightning, She wore high-heeled shoes and a crisp, white lab coat, a stark contrast to her chocolate brown hair. She sat in front of me on another of those doctors' rolling stools and explained my diagnosis and my options for treatment. The words rushed past me as I felt myself sink into familiar numbness. Somehow, I held on enough to hear and grasp what she said.

"For endometrial cancer, radiation can be applied in two different ways. Using external radiation, we aim radioactive beams directly at your pelvic region, the area where the cancer is most likely to recur. You would do this as an outpatient five days a week for four weeks. The other option, and the one I prefer, is high-dose brachytherapy. That's a form of internal radiotherapy where we insert a device into the vagina that delivers radiation directly to the area where cancer cells are most likely to form. Each brachytherapy session takes a few minutes, and you'd probably need three sessions."

Doctor U. briefly explained possible side effects of both procedures and then, "—Excuse me for a few minutes," she announced. "I have someone on the table, and I have to check on her."

She rushed out of the room leaving me there to ponder my options. I had no idea then which of them was the best choice or even if I should pursue preventative radiation. I needed lots more information before I could make up my mind.

When Doctor U. returned, I was grateful that she seemed calmer and more open to having a discussion.

"Do I really need preventative radiation?" I asked. "Everything I've read is confusing."

She wheeled herself on the stool to a computer that sat on a nearby countertop. I waited while she typed in a password and navigated to a screen that held information about adjuvant radiation treatment for endometrial cancer.

"Your situation is somewhat unique, because the tumor is exactly at the center of the myometrium." She clicked on a page that showed an illustration of a uterus, and she pointed to where my tumor had been. "How do we treat you? It used to be that we always recommended radiation for stage 1C, but that isn't true anymore. Newer research shows that there isn't much difference in recurrence between women who receive the radiation and those who don't." She brushed back her shoulder-length hair and looked at me expecting a response.

"That's exactly what I've been reading online," I said. "So what do you recommend for me?"

She took a deep breath and exhaled slowly while she looked at my chart. "Would I feel better if your cancer were clearly stage 1B or 1C? Maybe. Do I wish that there had been more nodes sampled? Probably. But the nodes they did take were clear." She hesitated. "There are differing opinions about whether or not preventative radiation is necessary for early stage uterine cancer. I think in your case, the choice is up to you. But if you want the brachytherapy, then we have to do it soon."

I still felt befuddled. Flip a coin? How could I decide without any absolutes or certainties? "What if I decide not to have it and the cancer comes back?" I asked.

"Then we treat it with radiation. Most of the time, a recurrence is caught early, and often we can cure the cancer with radiation therapy alone. That's why you need to keep your appointments with Doctor Z. You'll be seeing him every three months for the next couple of years, right?"

"Every three months," I answered. I shook my head and sighed, "I don't know what to do."

Doctor U. shut down the computer and stood up. "Well, why don't you go home and think about it for a few days? Talk with your family. Then give me a call, and let me know what you decide."

Obviously in a hurry, she shook my hand and sent me on my way. I left the cancer center feeling negative and uncertain. I think Gail would have been disappointed with my attitude.

I don't always learn from my mistakes. While trying to decide, I went to the online uterine cancer forum again, the one with the horror stories. I searched the term "brachytherapy," and I discovered that many women struggled with the same decision I did. Should I have radiation or not? Most of the women were afraid, and I didn't find one response that reassured me that not having the treatment was a viable option. Reading their pleas for help brought me nearer to Neville, and I didn't want to go there. So, I logged out, and I did what I should have done before consulting the Internet. I asked myself, what would Jesus do when faced with a big decision?

I decided that Jesus would pray. The first thing He would do is pray.

As I knelt by my bed that night, I thought of Jeremiah 29:11: "'For I know the plans I have for you,' declares the Lord, 'plans to prosper you and not to harm you, plans to give you hope and a future.'" I prayed asking God to make His plans clear to me, to tell me which path I should take to arrive at the most harmless, prosperous, and hopeful place. During the next few days, I soaked my situation with prayer, and still I had no clear answer about which way to go.

Psalm 119:105 says, "Your word is a lamp to my feet and a light for my path." So I thought that God might speak to me as I read my bible. I even searched online to see if anyone had recommended specific scriptures verses or bible stories that might help me to make a decision, but I found none. I wished that in my bible concordance there were something that said "adjuvant radiation therapy." Not knowing where to turn, I read random scripture passages, but nothing leapt out at me.

Why was God being silent?

I decided to take that question to my friend, Susan. I admired her wisdom. God had blessed her with the ability to say the right words at just the right times.

"Maybe it doesn't matter what you decide," Susan suggested. "Sometimes, unless God clearly wants you to go in a certain way, He leaves the decision up to you. You've prayed, you've searched His Word, and you need to decide soon. What feels right to you? What do *you* think you should do?"

I realized that the answer had been with me all along. Somewhere deep inside of me I knew that radiation wasn't the right choice for me. My uncertainty came with thinking that maybe I didn't want the treatment because I was afraid of it. The idea of internal radiation isn't a pleasant one. But I didn't even know about that option until Doctor U. had told me. My body had been through a lot already, and I didn't want to put it through anything more unless it was absolutely necessary for my healing. Like The Woman With The Issue Of Blood, I had left my bleeding in the past, and I had returned to my camp. Neither Doctor Z. nor Doctor U. had said anything to convince me that I absolutely needed radiation therapy.

After my conversation with Susan, I shared my thoughts with

Sarah and Chuck.

"I don't think I'm going to do it," I told them.

We discussed what Doctor U. had said that there is conflicting information about adjuvant radiation therapy, and if the cancer did come back in the pelvic area it would be treatable with radiation. So, I decided against adjuvant radiation therapy. I stepped out in faith into the maze, confident that it would lead to the destination that God had chosen for me. I had made a choice that I was comfortable with.

In L. Frank Baum's classic book *The Wonderful Wizard of Oz*, the Yellow Brick Road is in disrepair. While Dorothy and Scarecrow travel it together, Scarecrow has a difficult time walking. I'll let Baum's own words paint the picture for you:

"After a few hours the road began to be rough, and the walking grew so difficult that the Scarecrow often stumbled over the yellow bricks, which were here very uneven. Sometimes, indeed, they were broken or missing altogether, leaving holes that Toto jumped across and Dorothy walked around. As for the Scarecrow, having no brains, he walked straight ahead, and so stepped into the holes and fell at full length on the hard bricks. It never hurt him, however, and Dorothy would pick him up and set him upon his feet again . . . The farms were not nearly so well cared for here as they were farther back. There were fewer houses and fewer fruit trees, and the farther they went the more dismal and lonesome the country became . . . There were no fences at all by the roadside now, and the land was rough and untilled. Toward evening they came to a great forest, where the trees grew so big and close together that their branches met over the road of yellow brick. It was almost dark under the trees, for the branches shut out the daylight; but the travelers did not stop, and went on into the forest . . .'If this road goes in, it must come out," said the Scarecrow," and as the Emerald City is at the other end of the road, we must go wherever it leads us.'"

During my diagnosis and surgery, I had traveled a similar

road, this one in dismal and lonely Cancer Country. I fell many times along the way, but Jesus picked me up. I walked along a road that was almost dark under the trees, a place where the branches shut out most of the daylight. But finally, I could envision coming out of the forest and into the light. The future lay ahead of me like the Emerald City, a future bright with hope in Christ.

After my conversations with Susan and Sarah and Chuck, God spoke to me through Proverbs 3:5-6: "Trust in the Lord with all your heart and lean not on your own understanding. In all your ways submit to him, and he will make your paths straight."

Every cancer patient has to find her own path to the treatment that is right for her. Please read that sentence again and let it sink in. Every woman must choose her own best option for preventative treatment, and for some women adjuvant radiation therapy might be what's best. But after much prayer and thought, I had made my decision. I called Doctor U. and told her, "No radiation."

It was time to move on.

CHAPTER 17
We're Not In Kansas Anymore

The day had begun with clear, blue sky and lazy summer sunshine, but by afternoon a veil of gray clouds had rolled in and shrouded the Kansas countryside. A far-away roar caught Dorothy Gale's attention. The noise rumbled toward her like a distant freight train.

Beyond the acres of wheat and cornfields, Dorothy saw dark clouds churning 'round and 'round, and then a sinister black tail dropping down—a swirling, dangling pillar. The cyclone wobbled forward sweeping the earth clean.

Terrified, Dorothy picked up her little dog, Toto, and ran for home. And as the whirlwind drew near, Dorothy hurried up the front steps of her small, shabby farmhouse and onto the porch. She expected the house to be safe and secure. But it was not.

She reached for the door handle just as the fierce wind blew it off its hinges. Then the wind tore apart the only place where Dorothy had ever felt safe. Home.

She stumbled into the living room, holding Toto tight in her arms.

"Auntie Em! Uncle Henry!"

But no one answered.

Dorothy ran to her bedroom, and there she stood near the window until its frame caved in striking Dorothy and throwing her onto her bed, knocking her unconscious.

When she awoke, Dorothy discovered that everything had changed. She found herself, and her little dog, too, in the Land of Oz, a peaceful place, yet strange and unfamiliar.

"Toto," Dorothy said. "I have a feeling we're not in Kansas anymore."

That scene from The Wizard of Oz describes perfectly my experience with cancer. My bright and sunny life had turned cloudy. The clouds grew dark and gathered into a mass that pursued me and might have won. My cancer knocked me unconscious, and after a while I awoke in an unfamiliar place longing for home. I searched for a path to take me there, and I found none. Cancer had left me caught in a maze of past, present, and future. My destination was no longer home as I knew it, but instead a new normal.

How often have you heard that phrase *a new normal*? It's all over the place these days. I searched for its origin on the Internet and got lost in a sea of ambiguity. I've decided to agree that the phrase was born in the economic crisis of the twenty-first century and bantered about by Wall Street trying to soothe its battered investors. A new normal. In other words—it's time to pick up the pieces and move on.

In their journeys, cancer patients discover places within themselves that they didn't know existed. Have you seen the animated film Over the Hedge? In it, one of the main characters Vern the Turtle says, "There are even places in my shell where I haven't been." It's that way with cancer patients. We discover places inside of us that we hadn't been to until we got cancer. We become more aware of the organs in our bodies where the cancer grows. We wander into dark tunnels in our souls and search for a way out. We get stuck in elusive nooks and crannies with ghosts from the past and demons in the present. Cancer patients ride an internal rollercoaster of joy, sorrow, despair, fear, hope, and faith. For some, the new normal becomes a lifetime of cancer treatment. For those of us lucky enough to be cured, the new normal is a future hidden from view. It is like we are set in the middle of a field surrounded by nothing but sky, pioneers in the Old West looking at the land and deciding what we will make of it.

As I searched for my new normal, I thought again of The Woman With The Issue of Blood. How might she have picked up the pieces and moved forward after Jesus healed her? Of course, we can only imagine.

In Luke 8:56, we read about what happened in the moments just after her healing.

Jesus went with Jairus to his house, and he raised Jairus' daughter from death. The verse tells us that the girl's parents were astonished. *Astonished*. The dictionary defines that word as *greatly surprised*. I prefer more colloquial definitions like, they were "totally blown away" or "it knocked their socks off" (although I doubt that they wore socks back then). Can you imagine how happy and relieved those parents were? Luke 8:56 tells us that Jesus gave the parents a command. "Her parents were astonished, but he [Jesus] ordered them not to tell anyone what had happened." Say what? Don't tell anyone about this astonishing, blown away, knock your socks off thing! I'm almost certain that they did tell, maybe not the specifics of what had happened in their house, but how could they keep it a secret when a crowd stood outside knowing that their daughter had died, and now she was up and walking around?

We don't know why, but Jesus sometimes told the people He healed not to tell. Perhaps it was because the crowds following Him were too large and He didn't want to incite a riot, or maybe He didn't want too much emphasis placed on Him as a man who healed the physical body when His ultimate purpose was to be our Messiah, the One who heals our souls and paves our way to heaven. Whatever His reasons then, today we are encouraged to tell of the wonderful things that Jesus does. I think this is what The Woman With The Issue Of Blood decided to do—she decided to tell about the astonishing thing that Jesus had done for her. Jesus didn't warn her not to tell as he had warned Jairus. Instead he said to her, "Daughter, your faith has healed you. Go in peace."

So, while all the commotion was taking place at Jairus' house, The Woman With The Issue Of Blood stood outside with the rest of the crowd, joyful and bewildered, healed of her condition and ready to tell the world. She probably was eager to head back to her camp and share the good news with her family and friends.

But remember, The Woman With The Issue Of Blood might have been kicked out of her camp. The law back then, the one we find in Leviticus 13:46, said that as long as a person was unclean, as the woman had been, "they must live alone; they must live outside the camp." How long had she been gone? How far had she traveled beyond the security of home? We can't know. But let's imagine that she had been away for a very long time—twelve years—as long as she had the blood issue.

It is reasonable that she had to search for her camp. People moved around a lot in Jesus' time, depending on where crops grew well and animals thrived. When she finally found home, it might not have looked the way she remembered it. The Woman With The Issue Of Blood might have found herself in a strange new place like Dorothy's Land of Oz—a place full of uncertainty. Did her family and friends rush to meet her, or did they approach her with apprehension, worried that she was still unclean, worried that they might catch her disease? The woman's life had changed forever.

One thing I've learned in my journey is that cancer changes relationships.

I made a conscious choice when I was diagnosed to tell my family and friends, and not only to tell them, but also to openly share my journey along the way. My reasons were clear to me. First, I didn't want the rumor mill to begin cranking out stories filled with half-truths. I've seen this happen too many times. A person's name and the noun "cancer," are connected by the verb "has," and the sentence ends there. The listener is left to make up the rest, and that's dangerous. I wanted my friends and family to know the truth about my condition. Second, I shared my cancer because I wanted support. As stubborn and reticent as I am about asking for help, I knew that my time had come to seek it. And finally, I decided to share my cancer journey because I hoped that it might help women like you who are concerned with uterine cancer. I wanted to provide you with a better understanding of the disease, its risk factors, symptoms, treatments, and even what it is like to have cancer and to move beyond it.

The responses to my openness have been mixed.

When I put the word out that I had cancer and was having a

hysterectomy, it spread like wildfire among my friends. Get well cards poured in from former coworkers and people I hadn't heard from in a very long time. That was nice. I appreciated that they thought of me. But during my recovery when I really needed company, some of my friends backed off. Cancer makes people feel uncomfortable. Many don't like being around it.

One woman, bless her heart, brought food to me after I got home from the hospital. She didn't call before she came, but instead she left packages outside my door and then called me from her cell phone on her way home. "There's a treat on your front porch," she said. When I asked why she didn't come in to visit with me, she said that she had some errands to run. I understood. Some people just can't face Cancer.

Another friend worried that I might show her my incision. She announced when she visited me in the hospital that she wanted no part of that. (I hadn't intended to show her.)

Some people didn't want to talk about the cancer at all. If I brought up the topic, they changed it. Others were overly curious wanting to know if I still had any of my female parts or if my hair was going to fall out. These reactions didn't upset me. My friends meant well. My disease drew them close to their own mortality, and I understood that. Lord bless them for caring about me and doing what they could to support me.

That I'd had *uterine* cancer made some people even more uncomfortable. I discovered that for some of them cancers involving reproductive organs are unspeakable cancers. One of my friends couldn't believe it that I'd written a letter to the editor of our local newspaper openly asking for our senators and congresspersons to support the reauthorization of Johanna's Law—a law that provides funds to increase public awareness and knowledge of gynecological cancers. "You actually put it in the paper that you had *uterine* cancer!" my friend exclaimed. And a pastor told me that I was brave to speak so frankly about my condition because "uterine cancer isn't something that ladies usually talk about." When I shared with a store clerk that I'd had uterine cancer, during a discussion about cancer-fighting foods, she asked if that's the kind of cancer caused by a sexually transmitted disease!

There were also friends who drew nearer to me in my cancer. I've told you about my Cyber Jesus friends. They were there through the entire journey, and they continue to pray whenever a checkup looms. And family members have been wonderful, and Karen and Linda, Sarah and Chuck, my writer friends, and even strangers on Facebook and Twitter.

The truth is that your camp is not the same after cancer. I think that The Woman With The Issue Of Blood might have discovered this, too. When she returned home, maybe she was astonished by how much things had changed. Perhaps she cried out to God using the words from Psalm 61:4: "I long to dwell in your tent forever and take refuge in the shelter of your wings." Like me, The Woman With The Issue Of Blood probably faced finding a new normal.

Life after cancer sends us looking for the security of home. We remember how things were, and we want to go back to that time before our lives were turned upside-down. But as the American novelist Thomas Wolfe wrote, "You can't go home again." Cancer leaves you searching for a new way to define "normal." It leaves you standing in an open field ravaged by the storm yet surrounded with possibilities and realizing that you need a blueprint to build a new house.

"Where do I go from here?" Linda asked me several weeks after her mom died. For many years, Linda had been caught in the web of her mother's cancer, first breast cancer, and later pancreatic cancer. In the middle of the worst of her mom's battle, I was diagnosed with uterine cancer, and several people Linda knew died of various forms of cancer. To Linda, it seemed that cancer was all around her. Now, her mom was gone, I was cancer free, and what remained were shards of her life that had existed before cancer became more to Linda than just a word.

"You'll find your way," I answered. "Just put one foot in front of the other and keep moving."

The task for Linda and me and others whose houses have been ripped apart by the cancer cyclone is to decide how to rebuild. And rebuilding begins with putting one foot in front of the other and moving forward.

One day, I visited with a friend while she baby-sat for her

five-year-old granddaughter. Little Marissa sat in the living room singing along to a music video on the television, a Christian DVD of children's bible songs. You probably know the song. It goes like this

The wise man built his house upon the rock
The wise man built his house upon the rock
The wise man built his house upon the rock
And the rain came tumbling down
Oh, the rain came down
And the floods came up
The rain came down
And the floods came up
The rain came down
And the floods came up
And the wise man's house stood firm.

Do you remember singing that song in Sunday School when you were little? Maybe your children or grandchildren sing it now. It's based on Jesus' parable in Matthew 7:24-27. That's the parable where Jesus says, "Anyone who hears and obeys these teachings of mine is like a wise person who built a house on solid rock. Rain poured down, rivers flooded, and winds beat against that house. But it did not fall, because it was built on solid rock." (CEV)

As Christians, we build our lives on Jesus Christ. He is the solid rock, our foundation. When we believe in Him and hear and obey His teachings, we can trust that nothing will destroy us. That doesn't mean that we won't sustain some damage, or that we will never know suffering and pain, but our foundation will never be swept away. Our foundation, Jesus Christ, remains intact as the starting point on which we rebuild. As long as we know Him and hold tight to our faith, we can rebuild our lives on the Rock.

It is an absolute certainty that God will help us pick up the pieces and rebuild our lives according to His perfect plan. But what if we don't know the Lord? Or what if we have lost faith in Him? Then what? The second verse of the song holds the answer:

The foolish man built his house upon the sand
The foolish man built his house upon the sand
The foolish man built his house upon the sand
And the rain came tumbling down
Oh, the rain came down
And the floods came up
The rain came down
And the floods came up
The rain came down
And the floods came up
And the foolish man's house went "splat!"

Jesus' parable continues: "Anyone who hears my teachings and doesn't obey them is like a foolish person who built a house on sand. The rain poured down, the rivers flooded, and the winds blew and beat against that house. Finally, it fell with a crash."

When we haven't a firm foundation in Jesus Christ, when a flood or cyclone or cancer comes along and beats our house down, we see nothing but an empty space where our house had been.

That's where Linda was after her mother's death, standing in an empty field looking out into emptiness. But what she didn't recall was that the foundation to her house was still there hidden beneath the rubble. She knew the Lord, but she was still angry with Him. Linda faced a choice about how to rebuild.

Agnostics, and even those who have never accepted the Lord, can still change their minds and choose to rebuild on solid ground.

The last verse of the bible song that Marissa sang tells how to pick up the pieces and move forward. It shares a promise for everyone who believes:

So, build your house on the Lord Jesus Christ
Build your house on the Lord Jesus Christ
Build your house on the Lord Jesus Christ
And the blessings will come down
The blessings come down
As your prayers go up
The blessings come down

As your prayers go up
The blessings come down
As your prayers go up
So build your house on the Lord.

Everyone affected by cancer has the choice of either rebuilding on sand or on the Solid Rock. Faith is the keystone to rebuilding. When we pray, believe in the power of Jesus Christ, put one foot in front of the other, and move forward, then the blessings will come.

But what can we do after the keystone is in place?

Rebuilding our lives after cancer also means rebuilding our bodies. Regular checkups with our doctors and following their advice is essential for keeping our bodies healthy. We cancer patients are unique. We've walked the walk. Now we have to walk the talk about preventing cancer. We wouldn't wish for anyone to go through what we have gone through, and if someone asked us, we'd tell them to take care of themselves to prevent cancer from happening and to go to the doctor at the first sign that something might be wrong. We have to heed that advice ourselves and strive toward keeping our cancer from coming back.

"As the saying goes, 'Exercise is good for your body, but religion helps you in every way. It promises life now and forever.' These words are worthwhile and should not be forgotten."

Worthwhile, unforgettable words indeed, found in 1 Timothy 4:8 (CEV). This verse reinforces that faith is the keystone, and we build our bodies upon it. It says that exercise is good for us. Of course, you already know that exercise is important. Everywhere you look, there are advertisements aimed at getting the weight off.

According to the American Cancer Society, there is a strong link between endometrial cancer and obesity, and their best advice to prevent uterine cancer is to maintain a healthy weight through regular exercise. Walking, running, playing sports, working out at the gym, whatever way you choose, exercise is a strong rebuilding block. When we set exercise on the foundation of faith, we begin to rebuild our house on the Rock, a house built to stand strong against disease.

Eating a healthy diet is another sound rebuilding block. Which foods make up the best cancer protective diet? This is another fuzzy area regarding the prevention of uterine cancer and cancer in general. There are many options for you to explore. You need to find the one that is right for you.

The American Cancer Society suggests a plant-based diet of vegetables, beans and whole grains. Other sources suggest that foods rich in antioxidants might help to prevent cancer, and there are ongoing studies about foods like green tea and tomatoes as cancer preventatives. Talk with your doctor or a dietician and also educate yourself about making healthy choices that might help to prevent cancer. According to the American Institute for Cancer Research, eating a healthy diet, exercising, and maintaining a healthy weight might prevent almost a third of common cancers.

No, fellow survivors, we're not in Kansas anymore. A cyclone named Cancer came along and knocked us into an unfamiliar place. Now it's time for us to rebuild.

Faith, diet, and exercise; these three things combined can start cancer patients on the path to a new normal. And we know this for sure: If we rebuild our house on the Rock, then we will have a strong fortress in which to weather whatever storms come along. The bible promises us so in Psalm 91:1: "He who dwells in the shelter of the Most High will rest in the shadow of the Almighty," and also in Psalm 18:2, "The Lord is my rock, my fortress and my deliverer; my God is my rock, in whom I take refuge, my shield and the horn of my salvation, my stronghold."

Moving beyond cancer might seem overwhelming at first, but as we put one foot in front of the other, eventually we'll find the way home

CHAPTER 18
Bidding The Ghosts Farewell

*"LORD my God, I called to you for help, and you healed me.
You, LORD, brought me up from the realm of the dead;
you spared me from going down to the pit."*
—Psalm 30:2-3

I've had bouts of depression in my life, but none like I felt immediately after cancer. I'd left the physical trauma behind, still the emotional pain lingered. Depression came when I grieved for the carefree person I was before cancer and also as I watched others battle this insidious disease. In an odd way, I felt a loss of innocence. Cancer ambushed me and caught me unaware. I felt helpless while it ravaged me and then ran off. The attack was quick and yet so brutal and haunting that I looked anxiously over my shoulder wondering if it could happen again. The ghosts of Cancer stalked me.

Don't misunderstand. I was, and still am, grateful. The Lord blessed me with a cancer that was easily curable when caught early. My diagnosis and prognosis paled when compared to other cancers. Everything indicated that I was healthy again. My checkups showed no evidence of disease. Still, Cancer haunted me. It pulled me back to gray-veiled memories of the final days and the deaths of family members and friends whom I loved. Before Cancer struck, I could bury elusive thoughts of my own mortality. Then, Cancer made me face them head on. I am no longer able to stuff the idea that I don't have control over how long I live. Jesus promised me eternal life in heaven, but not here on Earth.

In our youth, it's hard to imagine that we're mortal. If you are the parent of a teenager, then you understand what I mean. Youth comes with the delusion of eternal life. How many anxious days have you spent wondering if your teenaged son or daughter is contemplating some sort of bold and dangerous act?

I remember hearing a pastor, Dr. Gregg Fletcher, speak about his daredevil teenaged son. The pastor and his wife never knew what feat Jake would attempt next, but most likely it would be some potentially life-threatening sport like extreme skateboarding, trickblading, or BMX biking. Then, one day, Pastor Gregg got the call.

"Hi, Dad."

"Hi, Jake."

"I'm going to be a little late for supper. Me and Dan are going to dive off the cliff at Gibraltar Dam."

"You're going to what? Jake!—"

"Gotta go, Dad. I'll call you from the other side."

The other side of where! Pastor Gregg dialed his son's cell phone number, but the call went directly to voice mail. He contemplated whether to jump in his Land Rover and drive down to Gibraltar Dam or to wait. He didn't want to upset his wife, Irene, so he strolled into the kitchen where she was checking on a pan of lasagna in the oven.

"Was that Jake?" she asked.

"Yes," Pastor Gregg answered, trying hard to act like nothing was wrong.

"Is he on his way home?" Irene wondered.

The pastor took several dinner plates from a cabinet next to the stove and began setting the table. "I guess so," he replied looking down, not wanting her to see worry in his eyes.

Then the phone rang.

Gregg's heart raced as he picked up the call. "Jake?"

"Hi, Dad," his son said. "Man, that was so totally awesome!"

Jake and his friend had dove from the cliffs at Gibraltar Dam and lived to tell about it.

Panic struck Pastor Gregg because unlike his son he had seen the aftermath of evil too many times. He understood that Evil lurks, taunts, beats, ravages, and kills. No one is immortal.

Our mortality is a topic that we don't like to think about. Many people including Christians are afraid of the idea of death, maybe not death itself, but the process of dying. How will we die, we wonder. Will it be painful? Will it take a long time suffering? Oh, that we could just have paradise here on Earth without having to transition to heaven.

In college, I took a course in Greek mythology. There I learned the legend of Aurora and Tithonus.

According to this ancient piece of fiction, Tithonus, a handsome, young mortal man, was the object of the goddess Aurora's affection. (If you're not familiar with Greek gods and goddesses, Aurora is the goddess of dawn who flies across the sky announcing the arrival of the sun.) Aurora's love for Tithonus was so strong that she wanted him to be around forever. So, she went to Zeus, the supreme god and ruler of Mount Olympus, and she asked him to grant Tithonus eternal life. Zeus agreed.

The couple lived happily together without any worries. But then, Tithonus began aging. His muscles turned to mush, his bronze skin paled, and before long Aurora was stuck with an average-looking, middle-aged couch potato instead of the handsome young man that she had fallen in love with.

After thinking about it for a while, Aurora realized that instead of asking Zeus to grant Tithonus immortality, she should have asked for his eternal youth.

There was nothing she could do about it.

Eventually, Tithonus's hair turned white, and he became skinny and feeble in mind and body. He roamed around Aurora's palace, clad in baggy celestial raiment and eating whatever he could of ambrosial food, until one day when his limbs were too weak to hold him up anymore. Then Aurora had no choice but to confine him to his chamber. There, Tithonus's feeble, little voice could be heard babbling and crying out to Aurora in the night.

"Aurora, my darling, where are you? Aurora?!"

When she couldn't take it anymore, Aurora found a creative way to end her lover's suffering. She turned Tithonus into a cicada—in Greek mythology a symbol of eternal life. In that form Tithonus lived on and on, chirping his way through eternity.

Man makes plans, and God laughs. When we try to cheat death, we risk ending up like Tithonus, stuck in a hopeless situation.

Today, there are all sorts of theories about how to stay young and live a long life, but the truth is that there is no eternal life on Earth. We all age, we all have an end story, and the only one who can grant us immortality is Jesus Christ. We have the promise of eternal life in heaven through believing in Him. None of us know how long we will live or how we will die, but we know that Jesus wants us to live life fully in our time here on Earth. In John 10:10, He says: "The thief comes only to steal and kill and destroy; I have come that they may have life, and have it to the full."

The thief, Satan, had failed to kill me, but in my weakness he tried to steal and destroy what was left of me. He worked hard to fix my mind on death, trying to convince me that cancer would take my life.

The panic attacks that I've suffered on and off throughout my adulthood became chronic about six months after my hysterectomy. I became almost housebound by anxiety, and I fought hard to do even the simplest tasks like drive on country roads and shop for my groceries.

The American Cancer Society reports that about 25% of cancer patients suffer from anxiety and clinical depression. I was one of them. Cancer combined with a series of other unpleasant events in my life had left me anxious and depressed. I saw a therapist, and I took medication. With help, I was able to recover. Most of all, belief and trust in the healing power of Jesus Christ brought me back. I've learned that although I don't have control over how long I live, I do have control over how I live *now*.

You've probably heard the little piece of scripture from the book of James that says, "Consider it pure joy, my brothers and sisters, whenever you face trials of many kinds." (James 1:2.) What James is saying there is to have a positive attitude.

How content we feel and how quickly we move beyond cancer and rid ourselves of its ghosts depends a lot on our outlook.

The first step in getting rid of the cancer ghosts is to change the way we think. Norman Vincent Peale, the well-known pastor, teacher, and author of the best-selling book *The Power of Positive Thinking* wrote: "Take charge of your mind and begin to fill it with healthy, positive and courageous thoughts."

His words echo what Paul says in Philippians 4:8-9, "Fix your thoughts on what is true, and honorable, and right, and pure, and lovely, and admirable. Think about things that are excellent and worthy of praise . . . Then the God of peace will be with you." Training the mind to think positively takes practice, and Paul tells us how. When the ghosts of cancer lurk and our thinking is muddled, we can ask, "Is what I'm thinking worthy of praise?" When negative and anxious thoughts overwhelm us, we can teach ourselves to replace them with other thoughts that are true, honorable, right, pure, lovely, and admirable.

After cancer, I work hard at staying positive by keeping a gratitude journal. Every morning, I write down one specific, positive thing that I thank God for. Then I meditate on that thing all day long, especially when Neville throws negative thoughts at me.

One morning, I wrote a blog post about a bad hair day. It began something like this: My hair went to seed last night, and wouldn't you know that my hairdresser is on vacation. I wonder, can I wait a week, or will I look like a musk ox by then? I meant the post to be light-hearted and funny, and most readers' comments added to the humor, but then I received this response from Liz, an old high school friend. *Just be happy that you have hair*. Liz is battling ovarian cancer and is undergoing her third round of chemotherapy. She hasn't experienced yet the joy that comes from a pathology report showing no evidence of disease. In the middle of her cancer treatment, she reminds us to be grateful for hair. Humbling.

There are so many unnoticed blessings in our lives—little things that we take for granted. In 1 Thessalonians 5:18, Paul reminds us: "Give thanks in all circumstances, for this is God's will for you in Christ Jesus." God wants us to always set our thoughts on gratefulness, especially when we find little to be grateful for. It is His will that we keep our minds focused on Him and His works, especially when the ghosts of cancer swirl around us. When we meditate on God, His works, and His words, we train ourselves to think positively. Isaiah 26:3 (ESV) says, "You [God] keep him in perfect peace whose mind is stayed on you, because he trusts in you." Peace comes when our thoughts are firmly fixed on the Lord and the ways in which He blesses us each and every day.

The second way that we can get rid of the cancer ghosts is to act on our faith. Like Dr. Martin Luther King, Jr. said, "Faith is taking the first step even when you don't see the whole staircase." Not acting can cause doubt. It keeps us stuck in the dark place. But, when we step out in faith and act like we've left cancer behind, we restore and build our confidence. There might be roadblocks along our new paths, and maybe we'll have to adjust our course a time or two, but any action is better than no action at all.

Do you remember the story in the Book of Matthew where Jesus walks on water? It's nighttime, and the disciples are alone in a wooden boat some distance off shore. A strong wind tosses the boat about and keeps the disciples from sleeping, and then, just before dawn, what do they see but a ghost walking toward them on the water. Of course, they are terrified. The bible tells us that they yelled, "It's a ghost!" But when the shadowy figure called to them, they recognized His voice.

"Take courage, it is I," Jesus said. "Don't be afraid."

When the ghosts of cancer haunt us, we can meditate on that image of Jesus walking on the water to remind us that there is nothing to fear.

The story continues with Jesus' disciple Peter deciding that he wants to walk on the water, too. So, in the darkness, he gets out of the boat and, wow, he walks on the water toward Jesus! Peter acts on faith, believing that he can. But then, he realizes that he's doing something scary and unfamiliar. He lets disbelief overtake him, and Peter begins to sink.

This might also happen to us when we start walking into a

new life after cancer. We might doubt that cancer has left us and feel ourselves sinking into depression. But hang on; there's hope. The story ends with Peter crying out, "Lord, save me!" and immediately, Jesus reaches out his hand and catches Peter, rescuing him from plunging beneath the waves.

"You of little faith," Jesus says. "Why did you doubt?"

When we begin to move beyond cancer and find ourselves doubting that we've left it behind, when we need help to keep moving forward, then Jesus will be there to save us. We'll never drown in a sea of doubt as long as we put our faith in Him. We'll keep going and keep on believing. We'll leave cancer in the past, and not look back. We'll say: "We *had* cancer. But we don't have it *now*." We will move forward in faith believing in the goodness of the path that God has planned for us. This is the way that cancer survivors move on. They act on their faith.

The third thing we can do to chase away the ghosts is to live life joyfully. Proverbs 15:15 says, "All the days of the oppressed are wretched, but the cheerful heart has a continual feast." If we allow our hearts to be oppressed, our days will be depressed, but if we fill our hearts with joy, our lives will be like a celebration. Another bible proverb 17:22 (AMP) tells us, "A happy heart is like good medicine."

Joy heals. It may not always heal our bodies, but it heals our minds. Even in the midst of joy-less, cancerhead times we Christians can live a joyful, happy life.

Some cancer hospitals use humor therapy, or laughter therapy, to relieve patients' emotional pain and stress. The American Cancer Society writes that laughter might release endorphins in the brain that help control pain. It also suggests that stress-related hormones can decrease during episodes of laughter. Laughter is good for our bodies. It increases circulation, exercises our lungs, helps relax tense muscles, and some studies show that it might even strengthen our immune systems. It pushes aside worrisome thoughts and replaces them with joy.

One of my former co-workers, a woman in her late thirties named Anne, suffered from metastatic breast cancer. The cancer came back several years after her initial diagnosis, this time in her liver. Anne continued to work during several rounds of chemotherapy. The drugs were administered 24/7 through a port implanted beneath her skin and into a vein in her body. A pump that Anne carried in a fanny pack delivered measured doses of the chemo throughout the day.

Anne loved to make fun of that fanny pack. She made silly covers for it, jeweled, leopard skin, and faux Louis Vuitton. She decorated it with feathers, plastic pink flamingos and bright-yellow smiley faces. Anne called the fanny pack her "bum bag," and she loved pretending that she had things hidden inside. One day, she stashed a small MP3 player in there that sent out sounds of a yappy dog! Through hair loss and all the other unpleasant side effects of her treatments, Anne always had a smile on her face. Understanding that her cancer made us feel uncomfortable, she found creative ways to put us at ease.

I asked her one day how she managed to find humor in her cancer.

"When you turn your face toward the sun," she said. "the shadows fall behind you."

I never heard Anne grumble or complain about her illness. On bad days, she was more quiet than usual, but she always managed to find joy in the smallest things.

Joy makes us strong, the prophet Nehemiah said. ". . .the joy of the Lord is your strength." Nehemiah 8:10. Anne found strength through joy, and her joy overflowed to us tenfold.

The word *joy* appears 165 times in the bible. In 2 Corinthians 7:4, Paul says, "In all our affliction, I am overflowing with joy." And in 1 Thessalonians 5:16, he tells us to "rejoice always." In Psalm 126:6, David says, "He who goes out weeping . . . shall come home with shouts of joy." The prophet Isaiah commands, in Isaiah 49:13, "Sing for joy, O heavens, and exult, O earth; break forth, O mountains, into singing! For the Lord has comforted his people and will have compassion on his afflicted."

The God-filled life is a joyful life because God is our Comforter and our Healer. When the ghosts of Cancer come at us, we know that we can chase them away with laughter and with joy.

Even with medication, psychotherapy, a sense of humor, and a positive attitude, I occasionally experience a "cancerhead" day.

These are days when memories of Cancer creep in and depression dulls my desire to be with people and binds my dry sense of humor. On those days I seek Jesus' companionship.

I imagine myself walking with Him on a path next to a quiet stream. We find an old wooden bench there, and we sit for a while. He reminds me not to be afraid of life and all that it brings. He tells me that wherever I go He will be with me in good times and in bad. Jesus always reminds me not to dwell on my end story but instead to look toward it with joy because it is the door to eternal life with Him in Heaven.

The ghosts of cancer are all about mortality. They make us believe that the end is just that—the end.

Years before I was born, my mother experienced a difficult pregnancy. The baby, a boy, died at birth, and Mom developed septicemia, blood poisoning. This is what she wrote in her diary:

"I was in a hospital room, in my bed, very sick, and the next thing I remember is floating out of my body. My soul left my body, and I was floating around near the ceiling. I noticed the time on a clock on the wall. It was a few minutes after 10 a.m. A doctor and three nurses were at my bedside, and I was looking down at them. 'We're losing her!' one of the nurses said. I heard the doctor order an injection of something. I can't remember what it was, but his voice sounded worried. At about the same time, I started floating into a dark tunnel with a bright light at the end of it. It wasn't at all scary. In fact, it was so peaceful and I felt such a sense of love that I wanted to stay there, but then I felt myself being pushed backward. It was like trying to walk into a strong wind. I crashed back into my body. I remember gasping for air, and a nurse putting an oxygen mask on my face. 'She's coming around,' I heard the nurse say."

Several years ago, when mom's end time did come, she faced it unafraid. While the process of dying wasn't something that Mom welcomed, she believed that death itself was nothing to fear. She had already been halfway there—and it was good.

Like most cancer patients, the ghosts of Cancer still stalk me, but now I have weapons stronger than theirs. On cancerhead days, I am able to fight against them with positive thoughts, faith, humor, and the belief that while cancer might someday be a part of my end story, it will not be the end for me. The truth is that I have no ending. I have been promised eternal life through Jesus Christ my Lord—and if you believe it, so have you.

Reader's Notes—Part Three
Use this page to jot down how you or a loved one might move forward into a joyful post-cancer life.

Part Four – Life After Cancer

CHAPTER 19
Guilt and Doubt

Two years have passed since I wrote the previous chapters. I had poured my words onto empty pages, and in doing so I relived my "issue of blood." The feelings that accompanied my writing had blended with the keystrokes, raw and intense. This was good because those unprocessed feelings allowed me to accomplish what I had set out to do—not just write a memoir about my cancer experience, but also help you see cancer as a journey of learning, faith, hope, and God's love. I had emptied all of that onto paper, and then I set the book aside. I felt emotionally spent and unsure of how to write these final chapters. For a while, I moved on. Cancer had left me, and I tried to leave it behind by fully surrendering the rest of my life to God. "Yet you, Lord, are our Father. We are the clay, and you are the potter; we are all the work of your hand." Isaiah 64:8. I knew that God wasn't finished with me yet, nor was He finished with this book.

As a survivor, I have come to view my experience with cancer as if I were a reporter working on an assignment. God sent me to a foreign land to live among its people for a short while. Then He brought me home and told me, "Now, share what you have learned." He didn't say what Jesus said to some of the people He healed: "Keep this to yourself" (although part of me would have preferred that). Instead, God told me, the one whose feelings were stuffed in The Hidden Place, to reach out and share my story with *you*.

So what have I learned? I know now that cancer is more about emotions—the soul—than it is about the body. Cancer pulls its victims inward to hidden places. It creates in them unfamiliar feelings and leads them to define who they are. When caught in cancer's throes, its victims cannot exist apart from it. An emotional war goes on inside of them, and they learn to live while fighting it.

I put cancer behind me grateful to be free of it, and gratefulness continues to be the most powerful emotion connected with my cancer. I am grateful to have experienced cancer because it deepened my relationship with God, and I am grateful to Him for freeing me from it. I thank Him every day for that. But with gratefulness, there also comes guilt. I seem to have beaten my cancer. Truthfully, I don't think about cancer every day anymore. But sometimes when I hear about or I pray for someone with cancer, gratefulness is flattened by questions. Why me? Why did God choose to take cancer away from me, but leave it with others? Guilt is common among survivors, and when survivor's guilt strikes me it sometimes revives memories of my friend Mark, a Vietnam veteran.

When Mark was nineteen, he volunteered to fight in a very unpopular war. He was a good man with a kind heart who battled an enemy that had no conscience. As an infantry soldier, Mark saw and participated in unspeakable acts, and for his bravery he earned three purple hearts and a bronze star. He served two tours of duty, and then he came home a changed man.

In reality the guns were silent, but still they resonated inside of Mark's head. He could not put out of his mind the men he left behind, and he carried their deaths with him for the rest of his life.

Mark never talked about Vietnam, not to anyone. He couldn't disconnect survival gratefulness from the guilt of surviving. In time, guilt was all that Mark felt. He fought a new enemy, Alcoholism, and he died of his addiction at age sixty.

Several men from Mark's platoon attended his funeral. They hadn't seen him since Vietnam, but they had traveled hundreds of miles to thank their old friend one last time. They shared stories about how Mark had inspired them and how he had encouraged them. When I remember Mark's Vietnam buddies saluting his casket as it was lowered into the ground, I think that nothing good comes of survivor's guilt. It draws us into ourselves and away from the Most High. Whenever I struggle with it I think of Mark, and I remind myself to soak up God's grace.

Last June, I received the good news at the doctor's office that I'd reached my third anniversary of being cancer free. I felt joyful as I went about my errands that day.

At the grocery store, I ran into a former coworker, an older gentleman whom I hadn't seen in many years. I had heard that his wife had inoperable cancer and was nearing the end of her life. When my friend saw me, the first thing he said was, "Jean! I heard you were sick. How are you? I hope that you're well now." I answered cheerfully that I had just passed the thee-year mark. He wrapped his arms around me, right there in the bread aisle, and he hugged me hard. "Oh, that's wonderful," he said. "Good for you!" When he released me from his big bear hug, I continued to feel the warmth and sincerity of his embrace and I felt overwhelmed, not by his affection but by guilt. He really was genuinely happy for me, but guilt kept me from soaking up the joy he delivered in that hug. I felt guilty that in the darkness of his wife's illness, this man had reacted and reached out to me with Light.

Survivor's guilt affects people differently. Some move forward searching for deliverance. They find it in helping others who suffer from cancer, or they join cancer survivors' groups and discover fellowship with like-minded people. They might seek individual counseling with therapists and pastors, and find answers through prayer and in the Word of God. But some, like Mark, keep their guilt locked away in The Hidden Place. Their guilt consumes them. They get stuck in it, and a few even transform their guilt into anger toward God. "Why, God?" they ask. "Why did you do that terrible thing?" They might blame themselves for someone else's suffering believing that it was caused by something bad they had done in their own lives. But clinging to false guilt and allowing it to fester is not how God wants survivors to live. God wants His children set free from Satan's counterfeit guilt. 1 John 3:20 says, "If our hearts condemn us, we know that God is greater than our hearts, and he knows everything." God knows that survivor's guilt is rooted in Neville's taunts, and God's will for us is to turn a deaf ear toward Neville and to find peace in the joy of our healing.

I have also learned that cancer binds its victims together for life. The Woman With The Issue Of Blood might say it this way, "Cancer creates a tribe." Some members of the Cancer tribe are ill and others are long-time survivors. They live together in this physical world, but emotionally they are worlds apart.

Some of you who are reading this book are currently battling Cancer, or you love someone who is. You remain firm in Cancer's grasp, and maybe reading my story of faith and healing is difficult because you want healing, too. During my cancer we faced some of the same challenges, fears, and heartbreaks. We were chained together for a while, like Paul and Silas in the bible, learning lessons that we might not have learned any other way. Then I was freed, and you were not. We are both members of Cancer's tribe, but our feelings are contradictory now. What I have experienced, healing, and what you are experiencing now still battling Cancer are at opposite ends of the camp. Neither of us is able to change that. But we live together peacefully in Cancer's tribe and try to love and help one another through the Love of Christ.

When I did research for this chapter, I visited the web sites of some of America's leading cancer hospitals. I read their articles about survivors' guilt and other post-cancer emotions. I also read comments that cancer survivors and their family members had posted.

One uterine cancer survivor shared that her cancer had been caught early, and she needed no treatment following her hysterectomy. But, at about the same time, her sister was diagnosed with stage-three breast cancer, and she faced months of chemotherapy. The sisters' feelings became an entangled mess of anger, joyfulness, and guilt. The uterine cancer sister felt guilty because her cancer was gone and her sister's wasn't. Her guilt deepened when she felt angry that her sister couldn't fully share in the joyfulness of her healing. The breast cancer sister felt guilty because she wanted to be healed too. She also felt unwelcome resentment toward her sister who was well again. She wanted to be happy for her sister's renewed health, but she couldn't find it within herself to genuinely feel that way. Cancer's emotional roller coaster affected the sisters' relationship so much that at a time when each turned to the other for support neither was able to give it.

Cancer, past and present, plays rough with relationships and it creates conflict within the tribe.

As cancer patients shift to cancer survivors they may not realize that their families and friends are transitioning, too. Family and friends are another part of the cancer tribe. They bear the brunt of caregiving. They provide a circle of support during cancer, and they, too, might find it hard to let go of their loved one's disease and move on. Cancer survivors want to leave cancer in the past, but with good intentions their support group might remind them to take things slowly or they may want to continue helping with shopping, housekeeping, or other tasks. Their ongoing worry and protectiveness clashes with a survivor's need for independence.

Also difficult for survivors is reconnecting with family and friends who backed away during cancer because they weren't able to deal with it. Anger, hurt, disappointment, and guilt are feelings associated with this sort of separation and they can lead to relationships completely falling apart. Too often, cancer related feelings are turned inward and left to smolder. Forgiveness is the key to reconnecting, and communicating about cancer is essential for tribe members to coexist in harmony.

Survivor's doubt is another strong post-cancer emotion. There have been times when Neville whispered into my ear, "Surely, you can't believe that God has healed you; He's given you a respite, maybe, but healed you? What makes you think that you *deserve* healing?" That didn't frighten me as much as it made me wonder if everything that I had learned on my cancer journey had really sunk in. If I had to face cancer again, would I react to it differently?

I received the answer last fall when I went for my annual mammogram. It showed a tiny, suspicious spot in my left breast. I felt worried, but not intensely worried like I had when I confronted cancer the first time. A second mammogram confirmed the small mass, and an ultrasound added that its appearance was characteristic of a malignant tumor.

When I heard this news, instead of retreating to The Hidden Place where my tears froze and I felt nothing, I remained in the moment and felt surprisingly calm. The next step was a needle biopsy. The calmness continued, and I was able to keep the worst-case scenario out of my head. "And the peace of God, which transcends all understanding, will guard your hearts and your minds in Christ Jesus." Philippians 4:7.

I didn't understand how I could feel so at peace while facing the possibility of cancer again, but I welcomed that peace and basked in it. I had learned through my uterine cancer to surrender my body to God. No matter what happened to it now, I was certain that my soul would be intact forever.

The biopsy came back inconclusive. The tumor was so small that the radiologist wasn't sure that his needle had pierced it. He referred me to a surgeon who recommended a lumpectomy. The surgeon said that if I did have cancer again, it was most likely not a recurrence of the uterine cancer. There are very few cases of uterine cancer recurring in the breast. So, if it was cancer, then it was probably a new unrelated malignancy.

Knowing this I still felt peaceful as I rested in God's unwavering love. "Lord," I prayed. "I trust you. I know that you are working out your plan for my life. Thank you for all the people you are putting in place to help me. When I'm in the hospital, please send your angels to watch over me."

Another surgery was more inconvenience than anything else. I had things to do and places to go. I felt irritated that I had to do this again, but I vowed to be cheerful as I headed into the pre-op preparation. Sarah was with me again, dear Sarah, and we joked and bantered about light topics until a nurse wheeled me into the operating room.

The outpatient surgery was routine and uneventful, and when I awoke in the recovery room, I felt no pain or discomfort. I rested in bed chatting with the nurse who sat at my bedside.

"What do you do for a living?" she asked, a standard question to see if my brain was fully awake.

"I'm a writer," I said.

"What kinds of things do you write?"

I explained that I write mostly for Christian publishers, devotionals and books.

She leaned toward me and gently placed her left hand on my forearm. Then, in a hushed voice, she asked, "Would you do me a favor, Jean? Would you pray for my dad? He has stage four liver cancer."

God wastes no time making connections among Christians. He moves us about like a scriptwriter writes characters in a play. Every stage direction, every word, is written with a specific purpose.

"I'll definitely pray for your dad," I said.

She almost whispered: "Is it okay that I asked you? I've never asked anyone outside of my family to pray."

Yea, God! Thank you for connecting us.

"Of course it's all right," I said. "I'll pray for you both. What's your dad's name?"

"Joseph."

"And your name?" I couldn't read her nametag without my glasses.

"It's Mary."

So there I lay in my post-op bed, possibly facing cancer again, and God brought angels—Mary, and Joseph by proxy—to my bedside. It doesn't get much better than that. Mary and Joseph got the prayer support they needed, and God lifted my spirits with a healthy dose of His humor.

I wouldn't be truthful if I said that I had no anxiety while I waited for the pathology report. My heart pounded steady and hard when the surgeon's office called and I braced to hear the words again, "Jean, you have cancer." Instead, I heard, "Jean, you're benign!"

Praise God! Praise Him not only for healing me again, but also for confirming my strengthened faith in Him. Praise Him with thanksgiving. Praise Him for choosing me to survive!

And as I praised God, Neville whispered his old, tired lines: "So, God healed you again? Don't tell anybody about it. It's selfish and narcissistic for you to feel so happy. And, hey, like I said before, this might just be a warning sign from God. Maybe your life will be one cancer scare after another. Maybe next time it'll be really bad cancer."

When survivors shout praises to the Lord for healing, Satan loves to shroud their faith with doubt and their joy with guilt. Guilt and doubt come from him. Any sort of false guilt is a lie. And Satan is the father of lies.

Why would anyone want an innocent person to feel guilty? Why would anyone want a healed person to doubt their healing? The answer is control. Satan wants to gain control over God's people, and one of the ways he does that is to wrap them up in guilt and doubt.

Cancer is our prison, and if God wills to set us free, then who are we to throw away His gift and stay imprisoned in doubt and guilt? Guilt and doubt do nothing to breed hope. They do not make us feel happy, content, or at peace. They stop us from rejoicing in God's goodness. They don't bring us closer to Christ nor do they help us to live in a more Christ-like way. False guilt and doubt are good for nothing. They pull our thoughts away from God's mercy and grace.

So, what steps can cancer survivors take to overcome post-cancer guilt and doubt? First, survivors need to evaluate any guilt they feel about their cancer and decide if it is legitimate guilt or false guilt. The guilt that comes with surviving cancer, whether our own cancer or the cancer of a loved one, is always false guilt. The bible calls false guilt "condemnation" (Romans 8:1). Satan loves to cause guilt through condemnation. That's why it's so important for survivors to avoid comparing themselves with those who are suffering or who have died. When survivors trust that their survival is part of God's perfect plan, then they can put away their own misplaced guilt and move forward with guilt-free faith.

Next, survivors need to work hard at turning doubt into trust. Benjamin Franklin said, "When in doubt, don't." Unlike cancer, doubt is something that survivors can control. The more that they learn to trust God, the less they will worry about what tomorrow might hold. Letting go of doubt permits survivors to live savoring each day as a gift from God.

Finally, cancer survivors can let go of doubt and false guilt by actively participating in their tribe, in other words, by looking outward and living life in a way that honors God and provides help and inspiration to others. The "Peace Prayer of St. Francis" offers excellent advice for how God wants survivors to live:

> Lord, make me an instrument of your peace;
> where there is hatred, let me sow love;
> when there is injury, pardon;
> where there is doubt, faith;
> where there is despair, hope;
> where there is darkness, light;
> and where there is sadness, joy.
> Grant that I may not so much seek
> to be consoled as to console;
> to be understood, as to understand,
> to be loved as to love;
> for it is in giving that we receive,
> it is in pardoning that we are pardoned,
> and it is in dying [to ourselves]
> that we are born to eternal life.

Dying to ourselves. This is how cancer survivors break free from all of the negative post-cancer emotions. When survivors give themselves to God body and soul, then they can bury their false guilt and doubts deep in the grave forever. They become right with God when they focus on rebuilding their lives on the foundation of Christ's love and when they live in a way that gives Him all the glory.

Cancer is a life-long journey. It changes the soul. It causes its victims to look deep within them and evaluate who they are and what is important. Cancer can strengthen faith if allowed to. It can teach valuable lessons about perseverance, hope, power, and peace. What cancer does in the soul after it leaves the body depends on the survivor. It can torment with guilt and doubt, or it can give fresh meaning to life and living.

CHAPTER 20
Blessed Are Those Who Mourn

Cancer helped me to learn empathy. Henry David Thoreau once said, "Could a greater miracle take place than for us to look through each other's eye for an instant?" This is what God has allowed me: an instant to look through the eyes of a cancer patient. He also allowed me to see that the patient isn't the only one who suffers through cancer. Families and friends suffer, too.

Family members, caregivers in particular, bear the heavy burden of cancer. They do what they can to help, but it is never enough because they cannot do the one thing that their hearts ache to do, bring healing to their loved ones.

Before I wrote these final chapters, I interviewed several people who had lost a family member to cancer. One of them was my friend Linda. It has been more than two years since her mother passed away, and I was curious to learn how Linda felt now. We met for lunch, and we sat in a booth at the back of the restaurant as far away from the other diners as we could get. I arrived with my little black notebook and a list of questions.

Linda and I hadn't spoken much about her mother's illness and death. Even before I began the interview, she told me that she had not shared any of what she was about to tell me with anyone. Linda was gracious and very open to being interviewed, and she seemed eager to share her feelings with me and my readers.

I began by asking her to think about the different emotions that she had felt during her mother's cancer and then to tell me about the strongest one. Without hesitation, Linda answered, "Anger." She looked at me hard, and she said the word with firm resolution. I noticed her body tense. She hesitated slightly waiting for me to say something, and in that brief moment of silence I sensed the flood of her emotions forcing themselves against a crumbling wall. I said, "Just talk. Tell me about who you are angry with and why."

"God," she said. "I was angry with God, and I'm still angry with Him."

The Lord whispered to me that He was giving me another chance with my friend. This time, instead of spewing advice, my role as an interviewer was to listen and not speak. This, I have learned, is one of the most important things a person can do for cancer patients and their loved ones—listen. Listen without judging and listen without offering unsolicited advice. Just listen.

Linda shared that her faith in God had crumbled because of an unanswered prayer. After her mother's first bout with breast cancer, Linda had begged God to keep cancer away from her family forever. Her experience with prayer had been that God answers yes, not yet, or I have something even better than what you've asked for. Now, God said no, and Linda felt abandoned.

"I'm surprised by how intense my anger was with God," Linda said. Then she offered advice to my readers, "Part of the healing process is to be angry. You are going to be angry, it's natural and it's okay to feel that way. Anger is necessary to heal from the loss, and you shouldn't try to stop or change that. Just let the anger run its course."

Linda is right. Anger is a natural part of the grieving process, and it needs time to work its way out. And that working out process is never easy. My friend reminded me, during our interview, that everyone experiences death and dying differently and grieves and heals differently.

"You can't compare yourself to others in your situation," she said. "You might be at a very different place than the next person and feeling different things."

Linda's words reminded me of something that had happened

in my own family years ago.

My mother told me a story about when she almost lost her life while giving birth to my brother. As I've written earlier, the baby died. This was eight years before I was born. Mother's doctor said that she probably wouldn't have another child, and in her story Mom revealed to me how Grandma Lily had reacted to the news.

Grandma went to the basement of the duplex she shared with my parents, and there she took an ax, and wielding it again and again she smashed a wooden cradle that had been in her family for many years. Grandma had slept in that cradle when she was a baby, and my dad had slept in it, too. Now, believing that she would never have a grandchild, Grandma Lily took out her anger on the baby's empty bed. She smashed it to bits, and then she gathered the wood, took it outside, and burned it.

My mother assumed that Grandma had smashed the cradle because Grandma was angry with her and blamed her for losing the baby. The two women had never really gotten along, and Mom felt that her mother-in-law was confirming that by destroying the heirloom bed. Mom held onto that belief forever without considering that Grandma might have been angry with God or even angry with herself. The issue remained unresolved. Mom and Grandma never talked about it. Communication was not something that my family did well. We made assumptions, and then we stuffed our feelings away to languish in The Hidden Place.

"On too many occasions," Linda continued, "people tried to tell me I should be here or there, or doing this or that, and that's not where I was. You have to be understanding with someone who's grieving. You have to be flexible."

And communicate and listen, I added silently.

Sometimes, we Christians run on ahead of God and say what we think we should say to a person who is grieving and has fallen away from their faith. I've been guilty of that with Linda. As the interview went on, I realized that what Linda needed most from me was to just sit there and let her talk.

The American Cancer Society offers advice about listening to help those who are grieving. They tell family members and friends, "Be there. Even if you don't know what to say, just having someone near can be very comforting. Listen and give support. Don't try to force someone if they are not ready to talk. Be a good listener. Accept whatever feelings the person expresses rather than telling them how they should cope with the loss, and never tell them how they should feel."

I've known Linda for thirty years, and we share much more than cancer; however, during our two-hour lunch we talked about nothing else. Linda said that it was good therapy for her to talk and to finally share what had been trapped inside her for so many months.

"What was the second most powerful emotion?" I asked.

"Guilt," she confided. "I wasn't able to tell my mom that I loved her." Tears came, and Linda wiped them away with a stiff paper napkin.

I couldn't just sit there and say nothing. "But she knew that you loved her," I responded. And then I asked my friend an Oprah interview question. Oprah is never afraid to ask tough questions. "Did your mother ever tell you that she loved you?"

"No," Linda answered softly. The waitress interrupted us then, and Linda asked for more napkins. We sat for a while until my friend regained her composure. "We never said 'I love you' in our family."

"But you know that she loved you," I continued, setting aside my interview in the name of friendship. "If, God forbid, you had been the one who died, wouldn't your mom have known that you loved her?"

"She would," Linda agreed.

I left it there. I was about to slip back into my old habit of giving unsolicited advice. I had empathy for Linda because I had also come from a family of non-communicators. We never said "I love you," either.

I remember the last time I saw my Grandma Lily. I had come home from college for a weekend, and Grandma had not been feeling well. She had suffered for a while from congestive heart failure, and that day she was extremely tired, pale, and not wanting to eat. She hated doctors and hospitals, but my dad finally convinced her that she needed to go to the emergency room. I stood on the front porch with her while Mom and Dad went for the car. As we waited for them to pull up at the curb, my grandmother extended her right hand toward me and I took it in mine. She shook my hand as if we had just met. "Good luck to you," she said without emotion. I felt her hand tighten around mine.

"You, too," I answered stoically, lightly squeezing her hand.

You might ask me, "Did she have dementia? Didn't she know who you were?" My answer would be no, she didn't have dementia. She was perfectly aware of who I was. Our parting reflected the way we had lived. No hugs, no tears, no I love you's. Love was something that we knew was between us, but we never talked about it. "Good luck." To both of us, this seemed a perfectly normal way to say goodbye even when we both knew that it might be our last goodbye.

The American Cancer Society also points out that it is normal in the period just before a person dies for family members and friends to withdraw, both emotionally and physically. This is called anticipatory grief. It helps prepare them for the loss. I think that withdrawal is even more powerful in families like mine who don't communicate well.

"There comes a time," Linda said, "when you realize that, no matter what, it is no longer in your control or power to change things. It is what it is, and it's at those times that you should say the things that you need to say. Tell [your loved ones] how much you love them and how much they mean to you. The void of their loss in your life will never be replaced, but knowing that when they died there was nothing left unsaid will at least give you a sense of peace. I had the chance to say things to my mom, and I never did...I still live with that guilt, and it hurts."

The bible tells us, "And we know that in all things God works for the good of those who love him, who have been called according to his purpose." Romans 8:28. If we have to be subjected to cancer, then at least we can find some good in learning from it.

Some cancer lessons are hard and unwelcome, but we carry them with us for the rest of our lives and they help make us strong. That day when I shook hands with my beloved Grandma Lily, I learned. My memory of us on the porch stayed with me, and as I matured I stopped holding back my feelings. My friends and family will tell you that now I am almost too open about what I think and feel. Some of them still cannot believe that I am writing about uterine cancer in such an open and personal way. But I would rather be open than to let my thoughts and feelings decay hidden inside my heart. I would rather tell you what I know about this cancer journey than to let you walk through it darkly.

Before writing this chapter, I did an Internet search of famous last words. I discovered that how we have lived has much to do with the ways that we die. Some people die angry. I read that the actress Joan Crawford spoke her last words to a housekeeper who stood at her bedside praying aloud. "Damn it . . ." Ms. Crawford said, scolding the housekeeper, "Don't you dare ask God to help me." Queen Elizabeth I died bargaining with God. Her last words were, "All my possessions for a moment of time." Leonardo da Vinci expressed guilt on his deathbed, "I have offended God and mankind," he said, ". . . my work did not reach the quality it should have." And others died saying simply, "I love you."

People seem to venerate a dying person's final words. Final words are held as a tribute, as a way of keeping a person's memory alive. But our own last words spoken to a loved one just before they die are private. We hold these words close and lock them away as a final remembrance. We keep them hidden like a faded rose pressed between the pages of a book.

I am grateful to Grandma Lily that I knew before my parents died that I needed to tell them "I love you." Still, I waited. I waited until I was certain that the end was near, and then I said the words, and my parents returned them. That brought me peace when Jesus came and took Mom and Dad home.

I wish that Linda had been able to say, "I love you" to her mother, not because it needed to be said, but because Linda needed to say it. It might have spared her from guilt and brought her some peace.

Neville loves to attack those who mourn. A grieving person is more than a target for him. He takes pleasure in using guilt and anger to pull a vulnerable, depleted soul away from God. But God is more powerful than Neville. He understands that anger and guilt mask intense pain, and He never abandons those who mourn. He waits, often just listening without giving advice. It may even seem that He's not there. But He is. Time heals, and God knows what to do with our time.

"Do you still believe in God?" I asked Linda.

She sipped her coffee and thought before she answered. I looked down pretending to study my notes. I wanted my friend to say yes, but I hoped that she wouldn't see it in my eyes. It was more important that I meet her where she was in her post-cancer journey than to make the same mistake that I had made while her mother was ill.

"I've never stopped believing," Linda said. "You can't be angry at something that doesn't exist. I still believe in God, but the forgiveness just isn't there yet. I guess my faith isn't as strong as I thought it was."

Linda went on to say that God had never left her. Even now, she still feels Him tugging at her heart. She has tried hard to ignore Him by removing remnants of Him in her home: a crucifix on the wall, a scripture plaque in her kitchen, an angel figurine. She has stopped praying, reading her bible, and listening to her worship CD's. But most of all, Linda has stopped speaking to God, and that is where she stands now in her journey through grief.

My last question for her was almost ridiculous. "How would you like to feel ten years from now?"

She had no answer. Mourning is like that. It tangles you up tight in emotions and then leaves you alone trying to free yourself. You can't imagine how you will feel a week from now, let alone ten years from now. All you want is to be set free and to know joy again.

Linda wonders if she will move beyond her feelings of anger, guilt, and pain. She believes that she might not. She thinks that the intensity will diminish somewhat over time but that the feelings will remain. Cancer has changed her. It has shown her a seedy side of life that she hadn't known. She told me that if she were to get cancer, she would go without treatment. She would give in to death without a fight. I think Neville would like that.

Earlier in the book, I wrote about Elisabeth Kübler-Ross's

theory of the five stages of grief. Written with the dying patient in mind, these stages also apply to close family members and friends. Let's take another look:

> Stage 1: Denial—This can't be happening to me or my loved one!
> Stage 2: Anger— Why did this happen to me, or to someone I care about?
> Stage 3: Bargaining— Usually with God
> Stage 4: Depression— I just don't care anymore. I can't take any more of this. I give up.
> Stage 5: Acceptance— I'm ready for whatever comes, or I'm ready to move beyond the pain.

Kübler-Ross's theory provides a starting point for empathy. It reminds us that a roller coaster of emotions is normal for someone who is grieving. If a person understands that, then he or she can meet their grieving family member or friend wherever they are in their journey toward acceptance.

I began this chapter by saying that cancer had taught me empathy. It has. I can relate to cancer patients, having been one myself, I share in the joy and apprehension that comes from surviving, and also, through Linda's words and others like hers, I can understand what life is like for family members and friends when their loved one has cancer.

Linda had one last piece of advice as our interview ended. "Tell people to communicate," she said. "Patients and family members try to stay strong for each other, and they leave things unsaid. It's not good when the end comes shrouded with lies. Whatever you need to say, whether it's good or bad, say it, and say it with love."

As Christians, it's hard for us to listen to Cancer speak without wanting to strike back with a sword and the armor of God. But sometimes, that's not what God wants us to do. He wants us to listen instead, not only to those who mourn, but especially to Him. Our merciful God knows that grieving takes time. He doesn't promise that He will always answer prayers the way that we want Him to, nor does He promise that He will answer all of our why questions. He does say, though, that people will know sadness and they will mourn. Jesus said it in His Sermon on the Mount. "Blessed are those who mourn." This confirms that in life God's children will know sadness. But then Jesus finishes his sentence with a powerful promise: "for they will be comforted." Matthew 5:4.

How long will a survivor's grieving last? Only God knows. In the bible when Joseph's father died, Joseph knew not to rush the stages of grief. He and the Egyptians mourned a long time (Genesis 50:3) Grief, in the form of anger, guilt or other emotions, can last for months and even years. To fully overcome grief, professional help through pastoral or other counseling might be needed. But no matter how long grief lasts, survivors can be certain of this—God will never leave them. If they trust in Him, even if they are angry and are not speaking to Him, God will find a way to comfort them and eventually heal their cancer-broken hearts.

CHAPTER 21
Final Words

Bleeding is a natural part of a woman's life. Thousands of years ago, the girl who would become The Woman With The Issue Of Blood got her first period. You and I reached that milestone in our lives, and so will the young women who come after us. For most, menstruation will be uneventful except for those joyful times when blood brings life into the world. For a few, menstruation will lead to an issue of blood, like uterine cancer.

In our journey together through the pages of this book, I've tried not only to inform you about the risk factors, diagnosis, and treatment of the most common form of uterine cancer but especially to share with you the emotions that come with each cancer phase. How a woman handles the emotions that accompany her cancer is just as vital as the treatments she chooses. Cancer is as much about feeling as it is about healing. It is an illness that the body fights by working together with the soul.

There are several powerful things that a woman can do as soon as she is diagnosed with cancer. The first and most important is to strengthen her faith in God and hang onto it unwavering.

The Woman With The Issue Of Blood is a biblical role model, a perfect example of faith. She persevered by believing that she would be healed. And like many cancer patients today, she spent all the money she had on doctors, and she suffered through treatments that didn't work. Surely, she felt frustration, grief, and anger. An issue of blood had stolen her normal life. It had most likely taken her away from her family. She may have felt guilt and blamed herself for not being able to care for her husband and children. Somehow though through the mess of her emotions she hung onto her faith. When she heard about Jesus, she went to Him not *wondering* if He could heal her but *believing* that He could.

The Woman With The Issue Of Blood is a loyal traveling companion for women diagnosed with uterine cancer. Whenever faith slips away they can read her story in Matthew 9:20-22, Mark 5:25-34, and Luke 8:43-47, and she will always lead them back to Christ.

One of the cancer survivors whom I interviewed, an agnostic, told me that she overcame cancer by having faith in herself. "I just told myself that I was going to beat it, and then I did," she said, matter-of-factly.

"But what if you hadn't beat it?" I asked.

She thought for a few seconds, shrugged her shoulders, and said, "Oh, well. There's only so much that I can do."

It's true. There is only so much that a human being can do. Jesus says in Mark 11:22 to have faith in God. Ephesians 2:8 reminds us that faith comes not from ourselves, but from the Lord. I can't help but wonder if that woman would have the same attitude if her cancer hadn't been cured. We try to be strong against cancer, but when our own strength is not enough then what?

Along with the believing kind of faith, there comes another means of coping with cancer—hope.

In Psalm 39, David writes about feeling hopeless. He begs God for help. We don't know exactly what problem David is facing but we know that he's weeping as he writes this psalm. Like my friend Linda, David believes that God is punishing Him by trapping him in a deep valley of emotional pain. He pleads with God to take away the suffering. He tells God that he just wants to enjoy life again. David might even be angry with his Heavenly Father. In verse 7, he says the equivalent of, "So, what do I do now, God?" Obviously, David feels hopeless. But then he answers his own question. He says, "My hope is in You." David surrenders his hopelessness to God. He acknowledges that on his own he can't climb the mountain of hope to get out of the valley of despair.

Jesus said that faith can move mountains. (Matthew 17:20.) Faith, the bible tells us, is being sure of what we hope for and certain of what we do not see. (Hebrews 11:1) When we surrender our hopeless feelings to God and put our hope in Him, then we acknowledge that God is capable of taking us to a place of restoration and peace.

When the Israelites felt hopeless, God spoke to them through His prophet Hosea. He said, "I will make the Valley of Trouble a door of hope." Hosea 2:15. David understood this. He knew that hope was his only way out, and he also understood that hope in himself was futile.

Along with faith and hope, a woman can fight cancer through prayer. Throughout the bible, we see examples of prayer unleashing God's power.

In Psalm 32, David encourages us to pray. In the same psalm God speaks to us through David's words, "I will instruct you and teach you in the way you should go; I will counsel you with my loving eye on you." Prayer is not only asking God for what we need, but also listening to Him. Sometimes, we get so wrapped up praying lengthy and involved prayers that we don't remain silent long enough to hear God speak.

I believe that one of the most powerful prayers we can offer is only four words long:

"Thy will be done."

Jesus included these words when He prayed in the Garden of Gethsemane. "Not my will, Father, but *thy* will be done."

It isn't easy to give up control of your life. It takes faith and practice until you can say, "Thy will be done," and really mean it. But, when you reach that point of surrender you will know it because in all circumstances you will feel God's love and protection, and He will bless you with an attitude of peace.

My mother faced her death with that sort of attitude. One

afternoon as we sat together in her hospital room, I asked how she managed to stay so strong. She said, "For most of my life I've started my day saying to the Lord 'Thy will be done,' and every night, I tell Him 'thank you.' In between, He knows what to do."

I'm sure that my mother asked God for certain things and hoped that she would receive them; however, she had unwavering faith that God would give her His best, and sometimes, for reasons that she wouldn't understand, His best was saying "no" to what she had asked for. Mom accepted that. She faced death peacefully with surrender and acceptance, and her example served as an inspiration to many.

There is another prayer, a well known one, that can help a woman get through the shock of a cancer diagnosis. It is the Serenity Prayer, attributed to the German-American pastor, Reinhold Niebuhr. You have probably heard it in its short form. Now, here it is in its entirety.

> THE SERENITY PRAYER
> God grant me the serenity
> to accept the things I cannot change;
> courage to change the things I can;
> and wisdom to know the difference.
> Living one day at a time;
> Enjoying one moment at a time;
> Accepting hardships as the pathway to peace;
> Taking, as He did, this sinful world
> as it is, not as I would have it;
> Trusting that He will make all things right
> if I surrender to His Will;
> That I may be reasonably happy in this life
> and supremely happy with Him
> Forever in the next.
> Amen.

Isn't that a perfect prayer for cancer patients? Acceptance, courage, wisdom; living in the moment, enjoying life, trusting God, surrendering to His will—all in a prayer less than 100 words!

Prayer is essential for handling the feelings that come with cancer. Prayer produces power. It yields healing as well as acceptance. I've seen, again and again, how cancer patients can rally as a result of intercessory prayer.

Another thing that a woman must do when facing a cancer diagnosis is to be informed. This means finding the correct facts in the right places. Those places include The American Cancer Society, The National Cancer Institute, The National Comprehensive Cancer Network, The Foundation for Women's Cancer, web pages of America's leading cancer hospitals, and, of course licensed health care providers.

A uterine cancer diagnosis is frightening and it leaves a woman not knowing what to do. Try not to rush to online forums and read posts by others facing your kind of cancer. You might find those web sites helpful to you later, but initially you need to know the facts, and you need to take things one step at a time and one day at a time. It is a common reaction for the mind to leap into the future and imagine what it might hold, but your mission is to work at staying focused on God and this moment and let Him worry about tomorrow.

The American Cancer Society predicted in 2013 that about 49,500 women in the United States would be diagnosed with uterine cancer. This includes not only adenocarcinoma but also all forms of uterine cancer. Of those 49,500 women, about 8,000 would die from their cancers. The average chance of a woman getting uterine cancer in her lifetime is about 1 in 40. And here is the most important fact to hang onto: there are 500 million women in the United States today who are survivors of this disease.

Each woman diagnosed with uterine cancer is unique. Her body, genes, DNA, general health, family history are all unique to her specific cancer. So, if you are diagnosed with uterine cancer, do not compare yourself to others.

Remember what David says to God in Psalm 139:13-16.

"For you created my inmost being; you knit me together in my mother's womb. I praise you because I am fearfully and wonderfully made; your works are wonderful, I know that full well. My frame was not hidden from you when I was made in the secret place, when I was woven together in the depths of the earth. Your eyes saw my unformed body; all the days ordained for me were written in your book before one of them came to be."

God has a specific plan for your uterine cancer journey, and He will work out that plan for you. He already knows your path and your destination, and it will be unique to any other.

Certain kinds of cancers get a lot of attention in the media. Uterine cancer has not been one of them. Most women can name the various forms of gynecological cancers, but they don't know the symptoms. The good news is that this is beginning to change thanks to The Gynecologic Cancer Education and Awareness Act, also known as "Johanna's Law."

Johanna Silver Gordon was a young schoolteacher and mother diagnosed with late stage ovarian cancer. She had been a health conscious woman who visited her doctor annually for pelvic exams and PAP smears, and when she began experiencing indigestion and abdominal bloating, she decided that it was nothing serious. Johanna was unaware that these were symptoms of ovarian cancer, and by the time she finally did see her doctor, she was shocked to learn the diagnosis. Johanna fought her cancer for 3 ½ years before she passed away.

Afterward, her sister, Sheryl Silver, proposed a bill to Congress that would work to educate women about the symptoms, risk factors, and prevention of gynecological cancers. "Johanna's Law" was passed in 2006 and renewed in 2010. As a result of this law, the Centers for Disease Control has created the "Inside Knowledge Campaign" to increase women's awareness through public service announcements, fact sheets, brochures, posters, and symptom diaries.

I urge you to spread the word about gynecological cancer among your family and friends. Don't think of this kind of cancer as something to be discussed in whispers. Awareness is the key to getting treatment early, and with early treatment many gynecological cancers can be cured. Don't remain silent! Be brave. Discuss gynecological cancer as freely as you would breast cancer.

I have said often in this book that communication is essential for cancer patients. Cancer emotions are like blending colors. Some mix together bright and beautiful, and others turn to ugly shades of brown and gray. Communication is much better than retreating to The Hidden Place, that place deep within, that cold, dark, unfamiliar cavern, that virtual tomb that I spoke of at the beginning of my story. Cancer patients, their families, and cancer survivors all need open communication, understanding, and support. Just like The Woman With The Issue Of Blood, they need a tribe that welcomes them fearlessly with open arms and hearts filled with God's wisdom and love.

As I write the final words of this book it is springtime in Wisconsin. Hyacinths and daffodils bloom and the air smells crisp, fresh, and clean.

There was a time when I hated spring. I especially dreaded April, the month when Easter most often occurs and all around there is the promise of new life. I hated April because its memories stirred my smoldering grief, a grief that at one time was so fiery hot that I ran from it afraid that it might consume me. Grandma Dorothy had died of cancer in April. My mother had died of cancer in April, and my father had died in April, too. These people whom I loved had all died within days of one another, although in different years. When I faced the possibility of uterine cancer in April, 2010, how could I not think that it would end in death? The feelings of fear that came with April had pressed solid against my optimism and faith, and in my cancer journey I struggled hard to fight them. Neville wanted me to be his slave again. He longed for me to sit imprisoned in my living room depressed while he berated me and tried to convince me that my headstone would be next in the family plot. Etched into the granite below my name would be the words DIED APRIL ___.

I fought against death and I won thanks to the grace, mercy, and power of my loving God. Today, I am alive, cancer free, and optimistic about my future. This is where I need to be now. God knows the rest.

I went to the cemetery last week. I visited Grandma Dorothy's grave and my mother's and my father's. Then, I walked up the hill to the angel statue. This time, instead of just looking at her I ran my hand over her face. I touched her single, frozen tear. I let my fingers slip gently down the sleeve of her robe, and I rested my hand on hers where it clung to the headstone etched with the name of the long-forgotten dear one. If I could, I would have pulled her hands away and released her from embracing that stone. She has grieved too long, and it is time for her to let go and move on. I don't think that I will visit her again.

Cancer has changed my life and changed it in a blessed and hope-filled way. Cancer strengthened my faith, and it brought me into an intimacy with God like nothing I have felt before. It taught me communication and surrender. Cancer deepened my prayer life, and it enhanced the way that I read my bible. I am blessed that my cancer was caught early, surgically removed, and is not likely to recur.

After I walked through cancer with God, the winter finally passed away, the storm clouds went with it, and spring came in its wondrous glory. By the grace of God, I have been able to leave death behind until that time when my Heavenly Father decides to call me Home.

In the classic book *Look Homeward Angel*, Thomas Wolfe's description of his character Eugene echoes exactly how I feel as someone who has survived cancer and is moving on. I hope that all of you facing cancer will someday feel this way, too. I leave you with these final words:

"And the angels...were frozen in hard marble silence, and at a distance life awoke, and there was a rattle of lean wheels, a slow clangor of shod hoofs. And he heard the whistle wail along the river. Yet, as he stood for the last time by the angels . . . he was like a man who stands upon a hill above the town he has left, yet he does not say "The town is near," but turns his eyes upon the distant soaring hills."

Reader's Notes—Part Four

Use this page to list how you might comfort a family member or friend who has lost a loved one to cancer.

ABOUT THE AUTHOR

Jean Fischer's writing career began as an editor at Golden Books. After several decades of writing for children, Jean now works as a freelance writer and consultant for various Christian publishers. Along with writing, she enjoys gardening, reading, and spending time in the great outdoors.

CPSIA information can be obtained
at www.ICGtesting.com
Printed in the USA
LVHW030340130720
660505LV00001B/194

9 781492 321354